ROUTLEDGE LIBRARY EDITIONS: THE ANGLO-SAXON WORLD

Volume 6

THE CÆDMON POEMS

THE CÆDMON POEMS

CHARLES W. KENNEDY

LONDON AND NEW YORK

First published in 1916 by George Routledge & Sons Limited

This edition first published in 2023
by Routledge
4 Park Square, Milton Park, Abingdon, Oxon OX14 4RN

and by Routledge
605 Third Avenue, New York, NY 10158

Routledge is an imprint of the Taylor & Francis Group, an informa business

© 1916 George Routledge & Sons Limited

All rights reserved. No part of this book may be reprinted or reproduced or utilised in any form or by any electronic, mechanical, or other means, now known or hereafter invented, including photocopying and recording, or in any information storage or retrieval system, without permission in writing from the publishers.

Trademark notice: Product or corporate names may be trademarks or registered trademarks, and are used only for identification and explanation without intent to infringe.

British Library Cataloguing in Publication Data
A catalogue record for this book is available from the British Library

ISBN: 978-1-032-52976-9 (Set)
ISBN: 978-1-032-54116-7 (Volume 6) (hbk)
ISBN: 978-1-032-54118-1 (Volume 6) (pbk)
ISBN: 978-1-003-41522-0 (Volume 6) (ebk)

DOI: 10.4324/9781003415220

Publisher's Note
The publisher has gone to great lengths to ensure the quality of this reprint but points out that some imperfections in the original copies may be apparent.

Disclaimer
The publisher has made every effort to trace copyright holders and would welcome correspondence from those they have been unable to trace.

Genesis in lingua Saxonica

US IS RIHT MICEL ÐÆT
we rodera weard. wereda wuldorcining.
wordum herigen. modum lufien. he is mægna
sped. heafod ealra heah gesceafta. frea ælmihtig.
næs him fruma æfre or geworden ne nu ende cymþ.
ecean drihtnes. ac he bið a rice. ofer heofen stolas
heagum þrymmum. soð fæst. 7 swiþ feorm. 7 wid bor
mahte. þæp æron geond gæste. wide 7 side. þurh ge
þeaht godes. wuldres beornum. gæstcu þæm dom.
hæfdon gleam. 7 dream. 7 heora ord fruman. engla
þreatas. beorhte blisse. þær heora blæd micel.
þegnum þrymfæste. þeoden his hæfdon. rægdon lus
tum lof heora lifes fruman. dugdon drihtnes 7 ge
þum. wæron swiðe gesælige synna ne cuðon. fir
ena fremman. ac hie on friðe lifdon. ece mid
heora aldor. elles ne ongun non. ræran on rodе
rum. nymþe riht 7 soþ. ær don engla weard. for
ofer hygde. þa lan ge opilse. no loan on dædgun lang.
heora selfra ræd. ac hie of siblufan. god es a
hwurfon. hæfdon gielp micel. þ hie wið drihtne
dælan mahton. wuldor fæpran pic. weroð
þrymmes. ro 7 þegl torhte. him þær sar ge lamp.
æfst 7 of er hygd. þær engla mod. þe þone un ræd.
ongun ærest fremman. þ þan ræc dan. þa he
forð we c pæð. riht of þuht ræð. þ heon norð dæle.

Fac Simile of the first Page of Cædmon.

Frontispiece.

THE
CÆDMON POEMS

TRANSLATED INTO ENGLISH PROSE

BY

CHARLES W. KENNEDY, Ph.D.

ROBERT STOCKTON PYNE PRECEPTOR IN ENGLISH
IN PRINCETON UNIVERSITY

WITH AN INTRODUCTION,
AND FACSIMILES OF THE ILLUSTRATIONS
IN THE JUNIUS MS

LONDON
GEORGE ROUTLEDGE & SONS LIMITED
NEW YORK: E. P. DUTTON & CO.
1916

Printed in Scotland by
MORRISON & GIBB LIMITED
Edinburgh

TO

L. B. K.

PREFACE

This translation of the Junius MS. was undertaken as a companion work to my translation of the poems of Cynewulf which appeared in 1910. The problems that centre in this manuscript are of such interest, and the poems themselves hold so distinctive a place in the beginnings of English poetry, that a complete translation of the Junius MS. has long been needed.

The Introduction contains a brief review of the critical studies that bear upon these poems, and an outline, at least, of the convincing evidence developed against the former theory that they could be regarded as the work of Cædmon. It has not been my purpose to offer new solutions of old problems, but to outline, as adequately and justly as possible, the various contributions that have been made to a knowledge and understanding of the Junius poems.

The translation is based upon the Grein-Wülker text. In a few instances, to bridge a break in the manuscript, I have used conjectural readings offered by Grein, not found in the Grein-Wülker text, and have called attention to such use in the foot-notes. The illustrative drawings which accompany the text of *Genesis* in the manuscript are reproduced in this volume, pp. 197–248. I am glad to avail myself of this opportunity to acknowledge my debt and express my gratitude to Prof. C. R. Morey of the Department of Art and Archæology of Princeton, who has contributed to this volume, as a preface to these reproductions, a critical discussion of the Junius drawings, pp. 177–195; and to my colleagues in the Department of English of Princeton, Professors G. H. Gerould, C. G. Osgood, and J. D. Spaeth, for valuable suggestions, helpful criticism, and generous interest in this translation.

C. W. K.

PRINCETON, *December* 1915.

CONTENTS

INTRODUCTION—

                                                          PAGE

    CÆDMON xi

    CÆDMON'S HYMN xxi

    GENESIS xxiii

    EXODUS xlviii

    DANIEL lviii

    CHRIST AND SATAN lxii

TRANSLATION—

    CÆDMON'S HYMN 1

    GENESIS 5

    EXODUS 97

    DANIEL 119

    CHRIST AND SATAN 147

THE DRAWINGS OF THE JUNIUS MS. . . 175

    PREFACE: THE ILLUSTRATIONS OF GENESIS . 177
        By C. R. MOREY, M.A.

    REPRODUCTIONS 197

BIBLIOGRAPHY 249

INTRODUCTION

CÆDMON

The name of Cædmon is for ever associated with the birth of Christian poetry in England. In a beautiful legend in the *Ecclesiastical History* Bede describes how Cædmon was magically blessed with the gift of song, quotes the hymn he sang when the power first came upon him, and enumerates the subjects treated in his poems. He sang, Bede tells us, " de tota Genesis historia, de egressu Israel ex Aegypto, . . . de aliis plurimis sacrae scripturae historiis." It was not, however, until the beginning of the second quarter of the seventeenth century that any poems, aside from the *Hymn*, were definitely associated with the name of Cædmon. About 1630 a manuscript, later known as the Junius manuscript, was discovered by Archbishop Ussher, and by him presented to Francis Dujon of Leyden, librarian to Lord Arundel, and known in literature as Junius. This manuscript contained the four poems, *Genesis*, *Exodus*, *Daniel*, and *Christ and Satan*. The manuscript is divided, however, into two parts only, each in form a single poem. *Genesis*, *Exodus*, and *Daniel* are written as one poem of fifty-five sections, *Christ and Satan* as one poem of twelve sections. Because of a slight correspondence between the opening lines of Cædmon's *Hymn*, quoted by Bede, and the opening lines of *Genesis*, the first poem in this manuscript, and because also of a partial correspondence between the subjects of Cædmon's poems which Bede mentions and the Biblical themes of the poems in the Junius manuscript, the four poems contained in this manuscript were soon accredited to Cædmon, and the whole was known as Cædmon's " Paraphrase."

An edition of the " Paraphrase " was printed by Junius at Amsterdam in 1655, and the manuscript itself was returned to England and later, with other manuscripts of Junius, lodged in the Bodleian Library at Oxford, where it is known as MS. Junius XI. It measures 12¾ in. by 7¾ in., is somewhat marred by missing folios, and is bound in vellum-covered oak boards, a binding dating apparently from the third quarter of the fifteenth century. The first part of the manuscript containing the *Genesis, Exodus,* and *Daniel,* written, it is believed, in a tenth-century hand, is accompanied by forty-eight crudely drawn but naïve and interesting illustrations.[1] The second part, which includes the various poems grouped under the title of *Christ and Satan,* is written in three different hands. The corrections in the manuscript show a fifth hand at work.[2]

Since the ascription of these poems to Cædmon

---

[1] See pp. 197–248.

[2] The Cædmon poems were collated with the manuscript by Sievers and the results published in 1871 (*Zeitschrift für deutsches Alterthum*, xv. 456–461). The following statement is there made by Sievers as to the handwriting of the manuscript: " Die handschrift des Cädmon ist nicht, wie bisher allgemein angegeben wurde, von zwei händen geschrieben, sondern von vier, deren drei auf den sogenannten zweiten teil, das gedicht von Christ und dem Satan entfallen. Von diesen letzteren schrieb die erste v. 1–124, die zweite v. 125–710, die dritte den schluss. Eine fünfte ziemlich gleichzeitige hand hat endlich die ganze handschrift durchcorrigiert."

the problems that have arisen, as scholars have attempted to secure definitive tests of the validity of this attribution, have been many and difficult.[1] This much is clear, however, that no critic to-day would be so bold as to assign the four poems of the Junius manuscript to Cædmon, or to any one poet. On the contrary, instead of criticism developing results that would link the four poems to one another, and to some one author, it has found in them evidences for belief that they must be assigned to somewhat widely separated dates, and to more than one author.[2] It is probable that in the *Hymn* we have an authentic poem of Cædmon. One would also like to believe, with Ten Brink, that possibly the *Genesis A* represents " a fragmentary and imperfectly transmitted work of Cædmon." The weight of evidence, however, is against this theory.

Aside from the four poems mentioned above, and the *Judith*, the ascription of which to Cædmon need no longer be considered seriously, only one poem has been attributed to his pen with any earnestness, and that on mistaken grounds. The *Dream of the Rood* was claimed for him in 1856 by Daniel Haigh, and his opinion was accepted and supported by Stephens in his *Old Northern Runic Monuments*. This attribution primarily rested, first, on the fact that verses from the *Dream of the Rood* are carved in runes upon the Ruthwell Cross, and secondly, on

---

[1] See Wülker's *Grundriss*, pp. 111–146.
[2] Balg, for example (*Der Dichter Caedmon und seine Werke*, Bonn, 1882, p. 44), believed that the poems of the Junius manuscript represent the work of at least seven authors.

the supposition that another bit of blurred and obliterated runic inscription on the same cross was to be interpreted "Cædmon made me."[1] As a matter of fact, no trace of the name Cædmon is to be found on the cross,[2] and there is no evidence that renders the theory of Cædmon's authorship probable. On the other hand, there is much evidence for believing that the *Dream of the Rood* is Cynewulfian.[3]

Although so much uncertainty surrounds the writings of Cædmon,[4] Bede has given us a clear and definite picture of the poet himself. According to

[1] A complete discussion and rejection of probability of Cædmonian authorship in the case of the *Dream of the Rood* is to be found in the Introduction to A. S. Cook's edition of the *Dream of the Rood*, 1905, pp. ix–xvii.
[2] *Die Nordhumbrischen Runensteine*, Vietor, 12.
[3] *The Dream of the Rood*, A. S. Cook, Introd. pp. xvii–xli.
[4] The name *Cædmon* is unusual, and its etymology has been the subject of dispute. The attempt of Sandras and Bouterwek to explain it as meaning "boatman" or "pirate" (*ced*, error for *ceol*) has been rejected. Palgrave (*Archæologia*, xxiv. 341–343) suggested that the poet may have been called from the Chaldaic name for the book of Genesis, "b' Cadmin." This view was opposed by Bradley (*Dictionary of National Biography*), who regards the name as an Anglicized form of the "common British name Catumanus (in modern Welsh Cadfan). The first element of the compound (*catu*, battle) occurs in the name of a British king whom Bæda calls Cædwalla. If this view be correct, we may infer that the Northumbrian poet was probably of Celtic descent." Cook in 1891 (*Modern Language Publications*, vi. 9–28), in support of Palgrave's theory, offers data tending to prove that "there was sufficient Oriental learning at Whitby, at some time during Cædmon's sojourn there, to admit of an intelligent bestowal upon him of an Oriental appellation." Wülker (*Anglia Beiblatt*, ii. 225–228) answers Cook's general argument, and offers evidence for the view that Cædmon is an Anglo-Saxon name.

Bede's account, Cædmon entered the monastery of Whitby under the rule of the Abbess Hilda, *i.e.* between 658 and 680. Bede tells us of Hilda that she was " nobly born, being the daughter of Hereric, nephew to King Edwin, and with that king she also received the faith and mysteries of Christ, at the preaching of Paulinus of blessed memory, the first bishop of the Northumbrians, and preserved the same undefiled till she attained to the vision of our Lord in heaven." [1]

At the age of thirty-three Hilda left the secular habit and shortly became abbess in the monastery of Hartlepool, in the county of Durham; and after some years of government over this monastery " she also undertook either to build or to set in order a monastery in the place called Streanæshalch (Whitby), and this work which was laid upon her she industriously performed; for she put this monastery under the same rule of monastic life as the former, and taught there the strict observance of justice, piety, chastity, and other virtues, and particularly of peace and charity, so that, after the example of the primitive Church, no one there was rich and none poor, for they had all things common, and none had any private property." [2]

The fame of Whitby, a double monastery, founded by Oswy, King of Northumbria, in 658, made up of a sisterhood of nuns and a fraternity of monks of the Benedictine order, under the governance of

---

[1] Bede, *Ecclesiastical History*, trans. A. M. Sellar, bk. iv. chap. 23.
[2] *Ibid.*

Hilda, has survived the ages undimmed. Ample testimony to the virtue and merit of her followers is found in the fact that five of the monks of Whitby were raised to episcopal dignity during the life of Hilda or soon thereafter.[1] Not the least of the glories of Whitby is its association with the name of Cædmon, who, according to the charming legend, within its quiet walls composed the first great Christian poems of our language with a sweetness and inspiration that fired men " with contempt of the world and desire of the heavenly life." Bede invests the story of Cædmon with naïve beauty and simple faith :

" There was in the monastery of this abbess a certain brother, marked in a special manner by the grace of God, for he was wont to make songs of piety and religion, so that whatever was expounded to him out of Scripture, he turned ere long into verse expressive of much sweetness and penitence, in English, which was his native language. By his songs the minds of many were often fired with contempt of the world, and desire of the heavenly life. Others of the English nation after him attempted to compose religious poems, but none could equal him, for he did not learn the art of poetry from men, neither was he taught by man, but by God's grace he received the free gift of song, for which reason he never could compose any trivial or vain poem, but only those which concern religion it behooved his religious tongue to utter.

[1] Bede, *Ecclesiastical History*, trans. A. M. Sellar, bk. iv. chap. 23.

For having lived in the secular habit till he was well advanced in years he had never learned anything of versifying; and for this reason sometimes at a banquet, when it was agreed to make merry by singing in turn, if he saw the harp come towards him, he would rise up from table and go out and return home.

"Once having done so and gone out of the house where the banquet was to the stable, where he had to take care of the cattle that night, he there composed himself to rest at the proper time. Thereupon one stood by him in his sleep, and saluting him, and calling him by his name, said: 'Cædmon, sing me something.' But he answered, 'I cannot sing, and for this cause I left the banquet and retired hither, because I could not sing.' Then he who talked to him replied, 'Nevertheless, thou must sing to me.' 'What must I sing?' he asked. 'Sing the beginning of Creation,' said the other. Having received this answer, he straightway began to sing verses to the praise of God, the Creator, which he had never heard, the purport whereof was after this manner: 'Now must we praise the Maker of the heavenly kingdom, the power of the Creator and His counsel, the deeds of the Father of glory; how He, being the Eternal God, became the Author of all wondrous works, Who being the Almighty Guardian of the human race, first created heaven for the sons of men to be the covering of their dwelling-place, and next the earth.' This is the sense but not the order of the words as he sang them in his sleep; for verses, though never so well composed, cannot be literally translated out of one language into another without loss of their beauty and loftiness. Awaking from his sleep, he remembered all that he had sung in his dream, and soon added more after the same manner, in words which worthily expressed the praise of God.

"In the morning he came to the reeve who was over him, and having told him of the gift he had received, was conducted to the abbess, and bidden, in the presence of many learned men, to tell his dream, and repeat the verses that they might all examine and give their judgment upon the nature and origin of the gift whereof he spoke. And they all judged that heavenly grace had been granted to him by the Lord. They expounded to him a passage of sacred history or doctrine, enjoining upon him, if he could, to put it into verse. Having undertaken this task, he went away, and returning the next morning, gave them the passage he had been bidden to translate, rendered in most excellent verse. Whereupon the abbess, joyfully recognising the grace of God in the man, instructed him to leave the secular habit, and take upon him monastic vows; and having received him into the monastery, she and all her people admitted him to the company of the brethren, and ordered that he should be taught the whole course of sacred history. So he, giving ear to all that he could learn, and bearing it in mind and as it were ruminating, like a clean animal, turned it into most harmonious verse; and, sweetly singing it, made his masters in their turn his hearers. He sang the creation of the world, the origin of man, and all the history of Genesis, the departure of the children of Israel out of Egypt, their entrance into the promised land, and many other histories from Holy Scripture; the Incarnation, Passion, Resurrection of our Lord, and His Ascension into heaven; the coming of the Holy Ghost, and the teaching of the Apostles; likewise he made many songs concerning the terror of future judgment, the horror of the pains of hell, and the joys of heaven; besides many more about the blessings and the judgments of God, by all of which he endeavoured to draw men away from the love of sin, and to excite in them devotion to well-doing and perseverance therein."[1] There follows in Bede an account of Cædmon's last sickness and peaceful death.

Marks of the miracle legend in Bede's account of Cædmon's inspiration need not lead us to doubt the essential veracity of his story. We may reasonably believe that an individual named Cædmon lived at Whitby while Hilda was abbess, and composed religious poems on the subjects mentioned by Bede;[2] that he was a layman without literary education

[1] Bede, *Ecclesiastical History*, trans. A. M. Sellar, bk. iv. chap. 24.

[2] The story of the Creation is a favourite theme in Anglo-Saxon poetry (see Brandl, *Englische Literatur*, s. 959, § 11), and references to it are frequent (see Klaeber's citations, *Anglia*, xxxv. 113). In one instance (*Beowulf*, 90 ff.) the poet outlines this theme as the subject of a gleeman's song, sung before Hrothgar in Heorot. For comment upon this passage, and an admirably thorough discussion of the Christian elements in the Beowulf epic, see F. Klaeber, "Die Christlichen Elemente im Beowulf" (*Anglia*, xxxv. 111–136, 249-270, 453–482, and xxxvi. 169–199).

until received into the cloister; that his poetic powers were first kindled by a religious impulse, and that shortly thereafter he turned monk. It is probable that Bede had read some, at least, of Cædmon's poems, and that his translation of the *Hymn* is a fairly faithful one.[1]

No more fitting spot could have witnessed this miracle of song than the "white town" upon the shore of the northern sea, sheltered by the Northumbrian cliffs sloping away to a wild moorland and overshadowed by quiet monastery walls. The atmosphere of the Northumbrian coast is widely reflected in Anglo-Saxon poetry, pagan and Christian alike. Men build their dreams with fragments of the realities they love or fear. The majesty and might of nature were felt as a challenge; reverential awe blended with fear, though a manly fear, of the unknown forms and powers of the natural world. Into alien themes creep bitter memories of the thundering might of the sea, the lashing of the winter gales, a realization of the feebleness of man in the presence of the unleashed powers of the world about him.

In *Exodus* the "desert terror" brooding over the grey heath through which the Israelites fled from their captivity was not alien to the oppressive, menacing silence of the Northumbrian moorlands. The path through the Red Sea was described as no gentle withdrawing of the waters, but a veritable building up of the waves into rampart walls, as if the mighty arm of God had cleft a "wondrous wave-

[1] Ten Brink, *English Literature*, trans. Kennedy, i. 371.

road" through the tumult of the Northumbrian breakers.

So in the quiet monastery at Whitby, as Cædmon bent over his parchment, the simple rhythms may well have blended with some echo of the surge and thunder of that northern sea, and from some eastern window the tossing ocean stretches, undulating from the far horizon to break at last against the Northumbrian cliffs, must indeed have been a mirror of dreams,

>"the image of Eternity—the throne
>Of the Invisible."

CÆDMON'S HYMN

In the process of destructive criticism that has gradually nibbled away the body of poetry first ascribed to Cædmon, the *Hymn* alone has endured challenge. In the case of this poem the weight of critical opinion is in favour of crediting Cædmonian authorship. The *Hymn* has been preserved to us, aside from the Latin version of Bede, in a Northumbrian version,[1] and in a West Saxon version in the English translation of Bede's *Ecclesiastical History*, which is usually accredited to Alfred. The question has of course been raised in connection with this hymn whether the Northumbrian poem, written at the end of a manuscript of Bede's *Ecclesiastical History*, is to be considered

---

[1] Cambridge University Lib. MS., Kk. 5, 16, fol. 128. Northumbrian version first published by Wanley: *Catalogus historico-criticus*.

an authentic poem or a translation of Bede's Latin version. Wülker[1] at first saw a difficulty in the way of accepting the Northumbrian version of the *Hymn* as the original poem of Cædmon which Bede was translating. Bede had declared that he was quoting the sense of Cædmon's *Hymn*, but not the order of the words. " Hic est sensus, non autem ordo ipse verborum, quae dormiens ille canebat." But the agreement between the Northumbrian version and Bede is so close that, supposing Bede's version to be a translation of the Northumbrian, it must be considered a faithful rather than a free rendering. Therefore it seemed, in the light of Bede's own words, that the Northumbrian could not be the original. Zupitza,[2] however, and Ten Brink[3] explain away this difficulty by the assumption that *ordo ipse verborum* in Bede is to be understood as meaning not merely " order of words " but " arrangement of speech," including rhythm, alliteration, and parallelism of synonymous phrases. In Wülker's *Grundriss*[4] he himself accepts this view. On the whole, the judgment of critical opinion has been that in the Northumbrian version of the *Hymn* we have a genuine bit, perhaps the only genuine bit remaining, of the work of Cædmon.[5]

[1] *Paul and Braune's Beiträge*, iii. 348–357.
[2] *Zeitschrift für deutsches Alterthum*, xxii. 210.
[3] *History of English Literature*, i. 372 ff.   [4] Page 120.
[5] In his interesting study of the Cædmon question, *Von Kādmon bis Kynewulf*, Berlin, 1913, Sarrazin returns to the former theory that *Genesis A* may have been written by Cædmon. In 1883 Ten Brink (*English Literature*, trans. Kennedy, i. 40)

INTRODUCTION

GENESIS

The *Genesis*, a poem of 2935 lines, comprises the first forty-one sections[1] of Part I. of the Junius manu-

suggested that possibly destructive criticism had already gone too far, and that "as regards the most extensive and leading poem of the manuscript (*Genesis A*), and this one only, it is quite possible that a fragmentary and imperfectly transmitted work of Cædmon lies before us."

[1] Numbered sections are a feature of Anglo-Saxon narrative poems, with the exception of the poems contained in the Exeter Book. In some cases these numbered sections seem to represent natural divisions of the poem. In other poems, for example in *Genesis* and *Exodus*, the numbered sections do not in all cases coincide with natural or logical divisions. In his article on *Beowulf* in the *Encyclopædia Britannica*, Mr. Henry Bradley suggested that "the sections headed with roman numerals in the MS. of that poem represent the contents of the loose leaves or sheets of parchment on which the poem was written before it was transcribed into a regular codex." He returns to this hypothesis in a paper read before the British Academy, 24th November 1915 (*Proceedings of the British Academy*, vol. vii.), and gives the results of a very careful study of the numbered sections in Old English poetical MSS. Mr. Bradley believes that he has proved sufficient uniformity in the number of verses and manuscript lines in the numbered sections of *Genesis A*, *Genesis B*, *Exodus*, and *Elene* (that is, uniformity within each poem), and produced sufficient evidence of a corroborative nature, to render it probable that the numbered sections "represent the separate sheets of the archetypal MSS." The same hypothesis, in his opinion, accounts for the division into sections of certain poems in the Exeter Book, a division indicated in that MS. not by numbers, but only by the initial capitals at the beginning of each section.

Bradley further maintains that the archetypal MSS. of *Genesis A*, *Genesis B*, *Exodus*, and *Elene* were the autographs of the authors of these poems. In Bradley's reconstructed division of *Genesis* and *Exodus* the former contains 43 instead of 41 sections, and the latter 9 instead of 8.

xxiv   INTRODUCTION

script. Certain linguistic, metrical, and structural peculiarities separate verses 235–851 from the preceding and following portions of the poem, as an obvious interpolation. These two divisions of the *Genesis* have come conveniently to be known as *Genesis A* (vv. 1–235, and 852–end) and *Genesis B* (vv. 235–851).

It was in 1875 that Sievers [1] made the brilliant suggestion regarding *Genesis B* which was destined to have so remarkable a confirmation. Calling attention to the fact that in places the vocabulary, syntax, and alliterative structure of the verse of *Genesis B* are Old Saxon rather than Old English in character, he stated that this interpolated passage was borrowed from a foreign source, and made the conjecture that *Genesis B* might prove to be an Anglo-Saxon version of an Old Saxon paraphrase of the Old Testament, perhaps by the same author as the Old Saxon paraphrase of the New Testament known as the Heliand. Portions of an Old Saxon original have since been discovered in the Vatican Library, and a dependence of *Genesis B* upon the Old Saxon version definitely established.[2]

We have therefore in the 2935 lines of *Genesis* in reality fragments of at least two separate poems.[3]

---

[1] *Der Heliand und die angelsächsische Genesis*, E. Sievers, Halle, 1875.

[2] See Karl F. W. Zangemeister and Theodore W. Braune, *Bruchstücke der Altenglischen Bibeldichtung*, Heidelberg, 1894, where an account of this discovery, a text of the Old Saxon fragments, and a consideration of their relation to the Anglo-Saxon *Genesis*, are given.

[3] See Jovy, " Untersuchungen zur altenglischen Genesisdicht-

INTRODUCTION xxv

The first fragment, *Genesis A*, an Anglo-Saxon poem, whether from the hand of Cædmon or not, describing in the first 235 lines parts of the Creation, is there broken off and the narrative resumed after the fall of man, continuing in free and expanded paraphrase of the Book of Genesis through the sacrifice of Isaac. The second fragment, *Genesis B*, an Anglicised version of an Old Saxon Biblical paraphrase, contains a second account of the fall of the angels, and the entire story of the temptation and fall of man. The joining of the two fragments is to be explained by the desire of a scribe for an unbroken narrative, and the opportunity afforded him to supply the missing material in *Genesis A* by inserting *Genesis B*. *Genesis A* is certainly older than *Genesis B*,[1] which can hardly be dated earlier than the first half of the tenth century, and is usually regarded as dating from about the middle of the tenth century.[2]

ung," *Bonner Beiträge*, v. 33-144. Jovy holds the opinion that *Genesis A*, as originally composed, was not a complete whole but a series of versified episodes. He believes that four sections—The Creation, 1-234; Banishment from Paradise and Murder of Abel, 852-1055; Noah and the Flood, 1253-1601; and the story of Abraham, 1701-2935—were composed by one author (p. 19). He regards lines 1055-1252, and 1601-1701, which contain the versified genealogical tables and the narrative of the Tower of Babel, as interpolations by a later author (p. 8). So also Balg.

[1] See *Englische Literatur*, by Alois Brandl, Paul's *Grundriss der Germanischen Philologie*, Bd. ii. s. 1090. Sarrazin ("Zur Chronologie und Verfasserfrage Angelsächsischer Dichtungen," *Englische Studien*, xxxviii. 170-195) regards *Genesis A* as the oldest Anglo-Saxon poem. Barnouw dates it at about 740 (*Textkritische Untersuchungen*, Leiden, 1902).

[2] A recent article by G. H. Gerould ("The Transmission and

xxvi INTRODUCTION

The *Genesis* is often described as a paraphrase of the Vulgate original upon which it is based. It cannot, however, justly be regarded as a paraphrase. Parts of the *Genesis* do indeed follow the Vulgate with some closeness; but wherever the poetic sympathy and imagination of the author are kindled, the theme is invariably expanded far past the boundaries of paraphrase. The description of the rebellion and defeat of the angels, the temptation and fall of man, the flood, the destruction of Sodom and Gomorrah, the battle of the five kings, and the sacrifice of Isaac, glow with true creative fire. The imagination of the Anglo-Saxon religious poets, when stirred, is often intense, conjuring up visions grim or lovely with a vividness that has power to startle.[1] But their imagination is also limited and insular. It cannot shake itself

Date of Genesis B," *Modern Language Notes*, xxvi. 129–133) proposes a date some twenty-five years later than this, and hazards the suggestion that the Saxon original of *Genesis B* was brought to England by the same foreigner who later, about the year 1000, wrote a Life of St. Dunstan.

[1] " The Anglo-Saxon poets seem, indeed, to possess true dramatic imagination. Thus, when Cain slays Abel, the poet, with the scene before his eyes, sees the earth soak up the blood as it gushes forth (*Gen.* 978–986, 1097, 1098). The episode of Noah's drunkenness is made more dramatic than in the Vulgate by the addition of Ham's laughter, which excites Noah's anger. The same thorough realization is shown in the expansion of Hagar's speech (*Gen.* 2272 ff.) ; and in the telling insertion that Sarah's laughter was *joyless* (*Gen.* 2380, 2381). The intended sacrifice of Isaac is vividly described—the fire is actually kindled (*Gen.* 2922)." A. R. Skemp, " The Transformation of Scriptural Story, Motive, and Conception in Anglo-Saxon Poetry," *Modern Philology*, iv. 423–470.

free from the moulding influences of the life immediately about of which it is a part. The sunshine and storm, the voices and the dreams of Anglo-Saxon England are inwrought on every page. All that lies beyond the foam-ringed shores of England the poet, by an unconscious adoption, has endowed with Anglo-Saxon character and life.

The religious themes of *Genesis* are remoulded by the poet, and stamped with the silent mint mark of their coinage. Much that is of Teutonic origin in manners and customs, character and feeling, is blended with the Biblical elements of *Genesis A* and *Genesis B* alike, and here and there, outcropping through an alien soil, are traces of the ancient pagan faith.[1]

There is a Teutonic flavour in the characterization of the patriarchs of *Genesis A*. They are delineated as great princes related to their people by mutual obligations of service and protection. The patriarch of *Genesis A* is called "folk-leader," "leader of the people," "leader of men." He is "guardian" of his relations, of his inheritance, of the kingdom, of the treasure. He is the "friend" of his people, the "joy" of his warriors, the "dispenser" of treasure, of gold, and of jewels. Loyalty to him is the great virtue. The Anglo-Saxon poet has in some degree vivified even the bare genealogical tables of the Vulgate by the addition of these characteristic Teutonic elements.

In the depiction of the warfare between the

[1] See *Teutonic Antiquities in the Anglo-Saxon Genesis*, C. C. Ferrell, Halle, 1893.

powers of good and the powers of evil the same atmosphere is evident. The angels are the vassals of God, as the devils are vassals of Satan. God is often referred to as the protector of His realm and His subjects. He is the "warden" of the skies, of the heavenly kingdom, and of mankind. He is the "keeper" of men, the "helm" of men and of angels, guarding them as a helmet guards the head. As a Teutonic prince is the "dispenser" of treasure, so is He the "dispenser" of life. The angels are His "thanes."

This Teutonic element is naturally strong in *Genesis B*, where it colours the relations between Satan and his followers. They are his "strong companions" and "comrades," "stout-hearted heroes." They have "chosen him as their lord," and "will not fail him in the strife." They are "stalwart warriors," "loyal of heart." The revolt of Satan and his followers against God is the violation of a feudal oath of allegiance to an overlord.

In the pagan battle poems of the Anglo-Saxons we are not surprised to find, with the eagle and the wolf, the ravens of Odin, the war-god, circling over the field of slaughter. But when the religious poet in *Genesis A* describes the armies of Chedorlaomer, king of the Elamites, and Amraphel of Shinar who was joined with him, and all the battle in the land about Jordan, the picture is conceived in the same Teutonic spirit, and the shadow of the birds of Odin flits between the poet and the sun: "Twelve winters long that folk had given toll and tribute to the Northmen, and would no more enrich the lord of Elam with their treasure, but they rebelled against him. Onward the hosts advanced, intent on death. (Loud sang the javelins!) Amid the spears the black bird, dewy-feathered, croaked in hope of carrion." After Abraham's victory and the redemption of Lot, far and wide upon the field of slaughter the ravens tear the bodies of the dead, and at last "rest upon the mountain slopes, gorged with the slain."

The raven likewise appears in the description of the Flood, but in this instance the author is merely expanding a tradition found in the Vulgate, viii. 7, and the expansion is not without parallel in Old Testament commentary. Noah sends forth a raven from the ark, "sure that in its need, if so be in its flight it found no land, the raven would return unto him again, within the ark, across the wide water. But," the poet continues, "Noah's hope failed him! Exulting, the raven perched upon the floating bodies of the dead; the black-winged bird would not return."

It is natural from its Saxon relationship that we should find traces of Teutonic mythology in *Genesis B*. There are two references in this poem to the "feðerhama" (fiaðrhamr) or magic garment of feathers, giving power of flight, associated with Freyja, Loki, and Wieland,[1] and akin to the *schwanhemd*[2] of the Swan Maiden myth. This word occurs in line 417, where the reference is to the flight of Satan's emissary from hell to earth, and in

[1] Grimm, *Deutsche Mythologie*, 4th ed., i. 272, 324.
[2] *Ibid.* i. 354–356.

line 669, where it is associated with the circling flight of angels about the throne of God. Also in *Genesis B*, line 444, we apparently have a reference to the " tarnkappe " of Teutonic mythology, the magic cap or helmet which rendered its wearer invisible. Satan's messenger, who is to undertake the temptation of man, is there described as making ready for the journey. " He set his helm of darkness on his head, bound it full hard, and fastened it with clasps."

The conception of hell that is reflected in the *Genesis B*, while based upon the teachings of the early Church, may also, in some degree, show an influence of Teutonic pagan tradition. Hell is represented as a deep abyss, surrounded by eternal night, filled with black mist [1] broken by tongues of flame, a prison of torture, a house of pain. It is a land of blackness without light, yet filled with fire. Here Satan suffers heavy bondage, chained to the floor of hell. " Bands of iron crush me down, the bondage of my chains is heavy. I am stripped of my dominion. Firmly are hell's fetters forged upon me. Above me and below a blaze of fire! Never have I seen a realm more fatal—flame unassuaged that surges over hell. Ensnaring links and heavy shackles hold me. My ways are trammelled up; my feet are bound; my hands are fastened. Closed are the doors of hell, the way cut off. I may not escape out of my bonds, but mighty gyves of tempered iron, hammered hot,

---

[1] Gloom is constantly emphasized in Anglo-Saxon poetry as a characteristic of hell. See *Genesis*, 42, 312, 333, 391, 392; *Christ*, 1543, 1642; *Fallen Angels*, 28, 38, 104–106, 111, 178.

press hard upon me. God hath set His foot upon my neck."[1]

But in addition to the "flame unassuaged" bitter frost and cold are also present as tortures.[2] "There through the never-ending watches of the night the fiends endure an unremitting fire. Then at the dawn cometh an east wind, and bitter frost—ever a blast of fire or storm of frost." In its details the picture of hell here drawn resembles the conception of hell usual to the Church Fathers, but the presence of the east wind and frost may possibly betray Teutonic pagan influence, and a half-memory of Niflheimr, drear realm of Hela, land of bitter cold and mist beyond the

> "ocean's northern strand
> At the drear ice, beyond the giants' home."

One can hardly consider, however, that the reference to cold as a form of torture in hell is at all a necessary or definite proof of Teutonic influence. As Becker has shown in his study of the mediæval visions of heaven and hell,[3] an alternation of heat and cold was one form of torture in the Buddhist hells. Reference occurs also to such alternation in the Book of Enoch, through which it may have found its way into the Christian Visions. Becker is inclined to believe that " the Anglo-Saxon poets, especially Cynewulf and his school, derived their

---

[1] *Genesis*, 371 ff.

[2] *Genesis*, 313. Cold is also mentioned as a form of torture in hell in *Christ*, 1547 and 1630 ; and in the *Fallen Angels*, line 132.

[3] *A Contribution to the Comparative Study of the Medieval Visions of Heaven and Hell, with Special Reference to the Middle English Versions*, Ernest J. Becker, Baltimore, 1899, pp. 10–11.

conceptions not nearly so much from the surviving traditions of Germanic mythology as from the writings of the Church Fathers. Their hell, therefore, is a purely literary product, with perhaps a very light background of tradition."[1]

The influence of the traditional conception of Satan upon the Loki of Teutonic mythology affords ground for interesting comparison. Bugge[2] in his consideration of these figures (pp. 73-83) derives the name Loki from Lucifer. With such derivation it is impossible, in his opinion, that there should not have been some influence of the traditional conception of Lucifer upon the genesis of the Loki myth. The traditional beauty of Satan or Lucifer, the light-bringer or morning star, not yet banished from heaven, came to be conferred upon Loki also. Both lived intimately among the gods. Both forfeited Divine favour and were driven out. Both, for their evil, were ultimately cast into bondage. Satan, in the traditional conception of the early Church, was bound both at the time of his ejection into the abyss and again in the harrowing of hell. Loki was bound after the death of Balder. There is, too, a certain correspondence of inward nature between the sly, mischievous craft of Loki, the fire-demon, and the grim, saturnine malevolence of Satan, who through the flames of hell-mouth " sendeth forth his ministers of darkness throughout the spacious earth."

[1] Becker, *loc. cit.* p. 64.
[2] *Studien über die Entstehung der nordischen Götter und Heldensagen* (German translation), München, 1889.

INTRODUCTION xxxiii

Of all the themes of *Genesis*, that which receives most expanded treatment, and is marked by fullest poetic power, is the account, in *Genesis B*, of the rebellion of the angels and the temptation and fall of man. In this section of the *Genesis* we are dealing with an episode which constitutes an Anglo-Saxon "Paradise Lost." The poetic narrative of that immortal legend is marred, it is true, by repetition, and marked, here and there, by crudeness that contrasts ill with the consummate artistry of Milton; but such crudeness as is found is rooted in strength, and it is the lasting glory of *Genesis* that the Satan, Adam and Eve of that poem endure comparison with the figures of Milton's creation, and now and again prove actually superior in greatness.

The problem has long been of interest to scholars whether there exists any direct relation between *Genesis* and *Paradise Lost*, whether Milton saw the text of the Junius manuscript, whether his knowledge of Anglo-Saxon was sufficient to permit his use of it, or, if not, whether the account of the fall of the angels and the temptation of man may not have been translated to him from the Junius manuscript by some friend.

In the first quarter of the nineteenth century suggestions that Milton might be indebted to *Genesis* began to be heard. Sharon Turner[1] first called attention to certain similarities between the two poems. Conybeare[2] notices the resemblance

[1] *History of the Anglo-Saxon.*
[2] *Illustrations of Anglo-Saxon Poetry*, by Joseph Conybeare, edited by his brother, W. D. Conybeare, London, 1826, p. 186 ff.

between parts of *Genesis B* and parts of *Paradise Lost*, and suggests that Junius may have spoken to Milton of the Cædmon poem. Wülker [1] in 1881 doubted any connection between Milton and *Genesis*. Milton's slight acquaintance with Anglo-Saxon, the fact that no acquaintance with Cædmon is evidenced in Milton's *History of Britain*, and a somewhat literal interpretation of Milton's line, "Things unattempted yet in prose or rhyme," constitute the arguments that led him to dispute any dependence of *Paradise Lost* on *Genesis*. Masson [2] speaks of certain "striking coincidences between notions and phrases in Satan's soliloquy in hell in the Cædmonian *Genesis* and notions and phrases in the description of Satan's rousing himself and his fellows in the first book of *Paradise Lost*. Very probably," he continues, "the coincidences imply only strong conception of the same traditional situation by different minds." Although Milton had been blind for three years when the first edition of the Cædmon poems was published in Amsterdam in 1655, nevertheless, since the Junius manuscript had been in Archbishop Ussher's library and had been given to Junius about 1651, and since Junius had resided continuously in London from 1620 to that year, Masson considers it "just possible that Milton had become acquainted with the precious Cædmonian manuscript before he was blind. If he heard of it, he was not likely to remain ignorant of its nature or contents."

[1] *Anglia*, iv. 402 ff.
[2] *Life of Milton*, vi. 557 note.

INTRODUCTION xxxv

Morley[1] and Gurteen[2] consider it unlikely that the Cædmon poems should have been printed for twelve years before the publication of *Paradise Lost* and Milton not know of them. Brandl[3] is of the opinion that correspondences exist between *Paradise Lost* and *Genesis B*, and that therefore *Genesis* may have influenced Milton in his conception of his theme. Stephanie v. Gajsěk, in a monograph[4] upon the relation of Milton to Cædmon, is strongly of this view, and attempts to prove definitely by similarities of style and parallel passages that Milton was influenced by parts of *Genesis*, and in particular by the characterization of Satan there given. This thesis can hardly be definitely established by internal evidence. There are too few parallels of really striking correspondence to prove the case. The possibility, however, remains.

The difficulty in proving definitely any dependence of Milton on the *Genesis* through the assembling of parallel or similar passages is that they may very possibly be correctly explained according to the hypothesis of Masson: "strong conception of the same traditional situation by two different minds." One who reads *Paradise Lost* with *Genesis* in mind will undoubtedly be conscious, now and again, of general similarity of idea or turn of expression. The speech of Satan in *Genesis B*, "This narrow

---

[1] *English Writers*, ii. 109.
[2] *The Epic of the Fall of Man*, London, 1896, p. 131.
[3] *Geschichte der altenglischen Literatur*, A. Brandl, Strassburg, 1908, p. 1090.
[4] "Milton und Caedmon," *Wiener Beiträge*, 35, 1911.

place is little like those other realms we knew on high in heaven," and Satan's words in *Christ and Satan*, " Farewell to earth and the gleaming light of day! Farewell the bliss of God, the angel hosts, the heavens above! " have apparent parallels in *Paradise Lost* (i. 75 and i. 242-257). The alternation of heat and cold as tortures in hell is, of course, also reflected in Milton (*Paradise Lost*, ii. 587-591 and elsewhere). The " home devoid of light and filled with fire " of *Genesis B* calls to mind at once Milton's

" Yet from those flames
No light, but rather darkness visible."

The real question in the case of such parallels is, however, whether they may not prove to be influenced by common sources or traditions, or whether they do not represent natural, independent, poetic developments of the same great theme.

The location of Satan's kingdom in the north of heaven in both poems,[1] for example, merely proves the knowledge of a widely current tradition by both poets. According to some systems of demonology the four quarters of the world, before the rebellion, were assigned to four angels, the north being assigned to Lucifer [2] in allusion to the words

[1] *Genesis B*, 274; *Paradise Lost*, v. 688-689.
[2] There is in the legends, however, a lack of uniformity in this assignment. In the " Faust Book," Beelzebub rules the north, and Lucifer the east. Hence Marlowe (*Faustus*, v. 104) makes Lucifer " prince of the east," while Shakespeare (*Henry VI.*, pt. I. v. 3) refers to Satan as " monarch of the north," and Greene (*Friar Bacon*, xi. 109) calls a demon Asmenoth " ruler of the north."

of Isaiah xiv. 12, 13: "How art thou fallen from heaven, O Lucifer, son of the morning. For thou hast said in thy heart, I will ascend into heaven; I will exalt my throne above the stars of God; I will sit also upon the mount of the congregation in the sides of the north." By Talmudic tradition, however, the sphere of all demons became localized in the north,[1] while the east was assigned to God, the south to the angels, and the west to man. The emergence of these same traditions in Teutonic mythology[2] makes it natural that they should be reflected in Anglo-Saxon poetry.[3]

A comparison of the *Genesis* with *Paradise Lost* is likely to bring forth as much that is interesting in divergence between the two treatments of the fall of man as in agreement. It is true that Satan is in each a titanic embodiment of strength and pride. And the Satan of *Genesis B* may in a real sense be called the hero of that poem. It is difficult for me to see how Satan can seriously be regarded as the hero of Milton's poem. The first few books might give some colour of plausibility to this claim, but as the narrative progresses it seems clear that Milton purposes to portray in the apparent heroic strength of Satan the destructive power of evil, a power so great that it consumes its agent as an acid

[1] Cf. also Jeremiah i. 14 and Job xxvi. 6.
[2] Grimm, *Mythologie*, iii. 836.
[3] In *Genesis B*, 274, Satan strives for a kingdom in the north and west. In *Genesis B*, 555, God's kingdom is located in the east, but in *Genesis B*, 667, Eve places it in the south and east. In Cynewulf's *Crist*, 899, the Son of God appears on Judgment Day from the south and east.

may destroy the vessel that contains it. So great is the scale of debasement from the form that

> "had yet not lost
> All her original brightness, nor appeared
> Less than archangel ruined,"

to the serpent form of the tenth book grovelling under the curse of a recurrent doom that all that once seemed heroic strength has vanished utterly.

There is a Teutonic strength in the very presumption and insubordination of the Satan of *Genesis B*. "Why should I toil?" quoth he. "I need not serve a master. My hands are strong to work full many a wonder. Power enough have I to rear a goodlier throne, a higher in the heavens. Why should I fawn for His favour, or yield Him such submission? I may be God as well as He!"

We are conscious of this same untamed and untamable strength even after Satan and his followers have been cast out from heaven and thrust into the abyss. As he lies chained to the floor of hell in torment, what sense of indomitable pride and will comes to us in that broken threat of the vengeance he yet might take in one short hour were his hands but free: "Alas! could I but use my hands, and have my freedom for an hour, one winter hour, then with this host I would—— But bands of iron crush me down, the bondage of my chains lies hard upon me." In the *Christ and Satan* we see the disintegration of this heroic strength, but through *Genesis B* it is a dominant note.

The character of Eve in *Genesis B* is less complex

than is Milton's Eve, and more appealing. As the whole temptation scene centres in her, the characterization of this figure necessarily affects the motivation of the scene. After Milton's Eve has yielded to the temptation of the serpent, and, desirous of wisdom, has eaten the forbidden fruit, she hesitates whether or not to make Adam co-partner in her sin :

> "Shall I to him make known
> As yet my change, and give him to partake
> Full happiness with me, or rather not,
> But keep the odds of knowledge in my power
> Without co-partnership ? So to add what wants
> In female sex, the more to draw his love
> And render me more equal, and perhaps—
> A thing not undesirable—some time
> Superior ; for inferior who is free ? "

What mistaken pride gleams in this last query of Eve, the creature of His hand " whose service is perfect freedom ! " But when she is most intent upon the retention of the advantages of sole wisdom there comes compelling thought of the penalty that likewise must be singly endured :

> " But what if God have seen,
> And death ensue ? Then I shall be no more,
> And Adam, wedded to another Eve,
> Shall live with her enjoying, I extinct !
> A death to think ! "

Nothing could be more different than the motivation of the whole temptation scene in *Genesis B.* Satan's emissary—Satan himself being bound and shackled to the floor of hell, helpless to stir—comes in his natural form, pretending to be a messenger from God sent to revoke God's former ban.[1] They are now to eat of the fruit which is no longer forbidden. There is a Teutonic touch in the fact that the fiend in *Genesis B* deals first directly with the man. "Hast thou any longing, Adam, unto God? I am come hither on His errand from afar." And it is a downright answer that Adam makes the tempter. "I know not that thou art an angel of the Lord from heaven. . . . Thou art not like to any of His angels that ever I have seen."

Then it is that the evil herald turns aside to where he sees Eve standing, and tempts her through her loving care for Adam, persuading her that he is indeed God's messenger, that Adam has given defiant denial to God's new command, and that only if she eat of the fruit, and persuade Adam to eat, can God's wrath be averted. "So he urged with lying, evil words, tempting the woman unto sin, until the serpent's counsel began to work within her—for God had wrought her soul the weaker—and she began to incline her heart according to his teaching."

[1] There is a reference in the text of *Genesis B* (line 491) to the assumption of the serpent form by Satan's messenger when plucking the apple of the temptation. The metamorphosis, however, was not, and could not be, maintained. From this point in the narrative the motivation of the temptation scene demands that the fallen angel speak in his natural form that there may be plausibility in his statement that he is a herald sent from God. The use of both forms is implied in the illustrative drawings of the Junius MS., certain drawings depicting a tempter of angelic form (see reproductions on pp. 209, 210, and 211), and others implying assumption of the serpent form (see reproductions on pp. 208 and 215).

At last Eve eats of the fruit, and, beguiled by a false discernment wherewith the fiend endows her, believes the deed to be good. She pleads with Adam to eat, lest he prove stubborn in disobedience: "Over and over the fairest of women pled with Adam until she began to incline his heart so that he trusted the command the woman laid upon him. All this she did with good intent."

The element of deception, as involved in the assumption of angelic form by Satan's messenger in the temptation scene of *Genesis B*, stamps the motivation as unusual, and such critics as Sievers, Hönncher, and W. P. Ker have credited this element in the *Genesis B* narrative to the originality and imagination of the Saxon poet. It is more likely, however, that the poet has introduced into his account of the temptation a more or less traditional motivation, found in apocryphal writings dealing with Adam and Eve. In the Latin *Vita Adae et Evae*, § 9, in order to persuade Eve to cease her penance in the waters of the Tigris, Satan assumes the form of an angel and announces to Eve God's forgiveness and the remission of the penalty. In the Greek *Apocalypsis Mosis*, in relating to her children the story of the Fall, Eve tells them that Satan appeared to her in angelic form, though she also refers to his speaking "out of the mouth of the serpent." We have, then, in this latter account the same confusion of motivation that exists in *Genesis B*, a confusion arising in all likelihood from an introduction into the Biblical account of the temptation in the Garden of a bit of motivation borrowed from the apocryphal version of the later temptation at the Tigris.[1]

From a philosophical point of view it cannot be denied that the motivation of the temptation scene, as given by Milton, is superior to that given in *Genesis B*. The action in *Paradise Lost* receives its great significance from its relation to the fortunes of mankind. Milton frequently directs the attention of his readers to the ages yet unborn. In the account of the Fall in *Genesis B*, on the other hand, the sympathy of the reader is primarily enlisted in the fate of Adam and Eve. The relation of their sin to those who shall come after them, though not wholly disregarded, is little stressed. The sin of Eve in *Genesis B* is not a conscious sin, but wrongful act resulting from deception. She is tricked into disobedience, the very sin she believes she is avoiding in persuading Adam to obey this new command. And whatever the nature of her act, we are left in no doubt as to the motive in which it originated. "All this she did with good intent." In Milton's account of the Fall it is the doctrine of free choice and the importance of spiritual perception that stamps the act of Adam and Eve as sin. Evil already exists in the world, and to man has been given power of choice to resist or to accept that evil.

"I made him just and right,
Sufficient to have stood, though free to fall."

[1] For a discussion of this problem see "A Note on the Sources of the Old Saxon *Genesis*," F. N. Robinson, *Modern Philology*, iv. 389–396.

Neither poem gives, as neither poem could give, a satisfactory explanation of the origin of sin in the mind of Satan. The appearance of sin in an innocent creation is simply referred back to its origin in heaven. The loathsome figure of Sin, self-begotten of Satan, springing a goddess armed from his presumptuous head, and her incestuous offspring, Death, represent the genesis of unpardonable guilt. The sin of Adam and Eve, depending in part upon the previous existence of evil, may be pardoned, and Paradise Lost issue in a Paradise Regained.

In all the magnificent frame of this universal drama it may be questioned whether Milton has at all surpassed the early poet in suggestion of the unstained beauty and innocence of a new creation. Through the pages of *Genesis B* breathes a childlike faith and trust, and the pathos of Adam's cry of repentance after his sin sounds in our ears with wistful sincerity and truth: "If I but knew the will of God, the penalty I needs must pay, thou couldest not find one more swift to do it, though the Lord of heaven bade me go forth and walk upon the sea. The ocean stream could never be so deep or wide that ever my heart would doubt, but I would go even unto the bottom of the sea, if I might work the will of God."[1]

An interesting detail in the structural unity of

---

[1] In these words of Adam, Robinson (" A Note on the Sources of the Old Saxon *Genesis*," *Modern Philology*, iv. 389–396) is inclined to believe that we have " a hint of the penance in the rivers, a conspicuous episode in the *Vita Adae et Evae.*"

Genesis A is the significance of the Cain legend as an integral link between the Fall of Man and the Flood. The banishment of Adam and Eve from the Garden was an arbitrary punishment. But in the slaying of Abel by Cain the guilty pair beheld the first organically inevitable punishment of their sin, the inexorable embodiment of the moral law of act and consequence. Of their own loins had they bred Death to punish their own sin. And the Flood, which is later sent upon the face of the whole earth to punish the evil which has arisen from intermarriage between the children of Seth and the monstrous descendants of Cain, is a link of equal organic validity in the chain of moral consequence. Despite the separated and somewhat scanty references to the Cain legend, it constitutes one of the most interesting themes in *Genesis A*. An excellent article upon the sources of the variant Cain legends and their literary recurrence, especially in Old and Middle English, was published by O. F. Emerson in 1906.[1] Brief reference to the material there assembled will be of value here.

The Cain legends, as extended in Hebrew tradition and early Christian writings, are moulded, so far as their reference to the birth of Cain is concerned, by a feeling, as Emerson puts it, " that something more than human depravity was necessary to account for such an extraordinary crime as murder in the comparative innocence of the early world." Rabbinical lore, therefore, makes Cain the son,

---

[1] " Legends of Cain, especially in Old and Middle English," *Modern Language Publications*, xxi. 831–929.

INTRODUCTION   xlv

not of Adam, but of the devil. According to other versions, Cain's nature was tainted by the influence of the time of his birth—namely, after the sin but before the repentance of Adam and Eve. The evil in Cain's sacrifice and God's abhorrence of it is likewise variously explained. The ill-will of his sacrifice, its unworthiness,—an offering of thorns and thistles,—the connection of the offering with the later law of tithing and the assumption that it represented false tithing,—these are some of the explanations offered for God's displeasure. The mark and curse set upon Cain are likewise variously interpreted,[1] but there is uniform stress upon the idea that the curse is an everlasting curse, and that Cain, therefore, may not hope ever to regain the mercy of God. In *Genesis A* Cain is "awyrged to widan aldre," accursed for ever.

According to the Scriptural version of the curse, he is condemned to be a "fugitive and a vagabond," and the ground is cursed for his sake, so that it "shall not yield her strength." Both of these elements are expanded in *Genesis A*. "Loathed of thy kinsmen, an exile and a fugitive, shalt thou wander on the face of the earth." And again, "The earth shall not give thee of her pleasant fruits for thy daily need. . . . Therefore the green earth shall withhold from thee her beauty and her delights."

[1] There is little English reference to the mark or sign that is set upon Cain. One hypothesis, that the sign consisted in a spasmodic trembling of the head, is given in the prose version of *Adam and Eve*. A second hypothesis, that the mark was a pair of horns, appears in the Cornish play of *The Creation*.

INTRODUCTION

No specific statement is made in the Book of Genesis as to the death of Cain. Tradition soon supplies such legends, however, and the poet of *Genesis A* has described the death of Cain according to the mediæval interpretation of the song of Lamech. This thread of the legend is treated in *Genesis A*, 1090–1103. " Then to his two beloved wives, Adah and Zillah, Lamech rehearsed a tale of shame. ' I have struck down a kinsman unto death ! I have defiled my hands with the blood of Cain. I smote down Enoch's father, slayer of Abel, and poured his blood upon the ground. Full well I know that for that mortal deed shall come God's seven-fold vengeance. With fearful torment shall my deed of death and murder be requited when I go hence.' " It will be noticed that all details are lacking in this version. In Baring-Gould's *Legends of the Patriarchs and Prophets* [1] some typical details are given.

" Now Lamech became blind in his old age, and he was led about by the boy Tubalcain. Tubalcain saw Cain in the distance, and supposing from the horn on his forehead that he was a beast, said to his father, ' Span thy bow and shoot.' Then the old man discharged his arrow, and Cain fell dead. And when he ascertained that he had slain his great ancestor, he smote his hands together, and in so doing, by accident, struck his son and killed him."

The monstrous descendants of Cain, and their relation to the Flood, is a further element of interest in the variant legends. In *Beowulf*, 111–114, occurs

[1] Page 97.

a reference to Cain's progeny: "Thence arose all monstrous births, eotans and elves and spirits of hell; the giants likewise that strove against God a long time; for this He gave them their reward." And again in *Beowulf*, 1266-1267: "Of him were born many demons; Grendel was one of them." Thus the descendants of Cain divide roughly into two kinds: first, eotans, elves, and demons; second, the giants. Of the first class *Genesis A* makes no mention, but there occurs an extended reference to the giant descendants of Cain. Since the deluge is sent to sweep away the evil they have caused, they serve as a direct link through Cain from the sin of the Garden to the Flood. "Then the sons of God began to take them wives from the tribe of Cain, a cursed folk, and the sons of men chose them wives from among that people, the fair and winsome daughters of that sinful race, against the will of God. Then the Lord of heaven lifted up His voice in wrath against mankind, and said, 'Lo! I have not been unmindful of the sons of men, but the tribe of Cain hath sorely angered Me. The sons of Seth have stirred My wrath against them; they have taken them wives from among the daughters of My foes. Woman's beauty and woman's grace and the eternal fiend have taken hold upon this people, who dwelt of old in peace.' An hundred and twenty numbered winters in the world that fated folk were busied in evil. Then the Lord resolved to punish those faithless spirits, and slay the sinful giant sons, undear to God, those huge, unholy scathers, loathsome to the Lord."

xlviii   INTRODUCTION

There follows immediately after this passage in *Genesis A* the account of the Flood. Perhaps in no episode of *Genesis* is the poet's imagination more stirred than here,[1] and nowhere does that imagination translate its chosen material more fully or more naturally into the familiar terms of Anglo-Saxon life. The ark, indeed, does not float upon the waters of a deluge, but drives through stormy ocean surges, as a ship flinging back from her bows the spray of Northumbrian waves. " Foamy-necked the ship fared on." True, it is spoken of as a " mighty sea-chest," as an " ocean-dwelling," and there is a reference to the " roof." But it is also a " vessel," " ship," " foamy-ship " with " well-nailed sides," and those who survive the flood are preserved within the " ship's bosom." The poet speaks of them as " wave-farers," " sea-farers " longing for " rest from their sea-journeying." The narrative attains a vividness, power, and fluency in the Flood episode not surpassed elsewhere in the poem. " Then the Lord sent the rains from heaven, and caused the black sea-streams to roar, and the fountains of the deep to overflow the world. The seas surged up over the barriers of the shore. Mighty in His wrath was He who rules the waters."

One of the most charming bits of verse in *Genesis* is found in this section in the description of the three flights of the dove from the ark. There is a tenderness in the poet's treatment of the theme which represents an essentially Celtic spirit. As

[1] *Genesis*, 1290–1500.

the dove goes forth in search of a resting-place and, finding none, returns and "settles hungry and weary into the hands of the holy man," we have a pleasant companion picture to that of the passage in *Guthlac A* in which Guthlac is welcomed to his hermitage again by the notes of the forest birds, which "were wont to fly in hunger round about his hand, in great desire, rejoicing in his succour."

In that part of *Genesis A* which follows the description of the Flood and has Abraham as its central figure, the poem becomes more and more a paraphrase, following its original with fair narrative accuracy, and a poetic power which increases, now and again, to a note of epic grandeur, as in the martial expansion of the account of Abraham's victory over the four kings contained in the 14th chapter of Genesis. But one feels that there is, on the whole, little attempt to organize into unity the heroic elements in the life-history of Abraham and little skill in subordination and emphasis. In the Offering of Isaac, it is true, we find adequate expression of the heroic strength of Abraham, and the poetic description of that great renunciation must have had for Anglo-Saxon ears an added element of reality in its hints of Anglo-Saxon life and custom.

The scene itself reflects the landscape of Northumbria, hills rising to a ridge of high land near the sea; and the details of the preparation for the sacrifice are suggestive of the Teutonic custom of building a funeral pile for a dead chieftain.

INTRODUCTION

The version of the Offering here given reflects the noble fervour, the religious passion of the poet. Unmarred by sentimentality, with unadorned austerity and power, the theme sweeps upward to the heights of tragic sacrifice. *Genesis* ends, as *Beowulf* ended, with the smoke of a funeral pile on hills that look toward ocean; but the death-wail of the pagan poem is replaced in *Genesis* by Abraham's prayer of thanksgiving for a son restored.

EXODUS

The *Exodus*, a poem of 589 lines, immediately following the *Genesis*, comprises sections 42–49 of Part I. of the Junius manuscript, but begins in the manuscript with a whole line of capitals, a usual scribal indication of the beginning of a new poem. As regards age, *Exodus* has somewhat generally been regarded as older than *Genesis A* and *Daniel*,[1] this judgment being based largely on the use of the article and the weak adjective, with some corroboration by the employment of metrical tests. On the other hand, Sarrazin,[2] on linguistic grounds, dates *Exodus* at about 740, and places it in the same period as *Beowulf*, regarding

---

[1] See *Geschichte der altenglischen Literatur*, A. Brandl, Strassburg, 1908, p. 1028.

[2] " Zur Chronologie und Verfasserfrage Angelsächsischer Dichtungen," *Englische Studien*, xxxviii. 170–195. See also Lorenz Morsbach, " Zur Datierung des Beowulfepos," *Nachrichten der Gesellschaft der Wissenschaften zu Göttingen ; Philolog-Historische Klasse*, 1906, p. 276.

INTRODUCTION

Exodus as later than *Genesis A* and *Daniel*, which he dates at about 700 or possibly earlier.[1]

Exodus treats, in its introductory lines, of Moses and his laws, his wandering, the plagues of Egypt, and the release of the Israelites. It then describes, in its main episodic divisions,[2] the march to the Red Sea, the pursuit by Pharaoh's army, the division of the waters and the crossing, the destruction of the Egyptians, the hymn of Moses, the rejoicing of his people, and the gathering of the booty. The poem is based in a general way upon the Vulgate Exodus or, more accurately, upon a

---

[1] Barnouw (*Textkritische Untersuchungen*, Leiden, 1902), assigns the following approximate dates for the poems of the Junius MS.: *Exodus*, 680–700; *Genesis A*, 740; *Daniel*, 800–830; *Christ and Satan*, 880; *Genesis B*, 1000.

[2] Napier has pointed out ("The Old English *Exodus*, ii. 63–134," *Modern Language Review*, vi. 165–168) that the episodic division of *Exodus*, as it stands, is confused because of a displacement of lines 86–107 and 108–124. This displacement, he suggests, may have been caused by "the wrong folding of a couple of leaves in the MS. from which Junius XI. was copied, or at any rate descended." (On this point see Bradley's "The Numbered Sections in Old English Poetical MSS." Reprint from the *Proceedings of the British Academy*, vol. vii. pp. 12–13.) As the text now stands the description of the pillar of cloud is followed by a description of the third encampment. Then occurs a reference to both pillars as if the pillar of fire had been already described. Then follows an account of the resumption of the march, but the narrative is interrupted by a description of the pillar of fire. Napier's suggested transposition of the two passages mentioned above (ii. 86–107 and 108–124) gives the following arrangement of episode: (1) ii. 63–67, second encampment; (2) ii. 68–85, description of the pillar of cloud; (3) ii. 108–124, description of the pillar of fire; (4) ii. 86–107 and 125–129, third encampment and march to the Red Sea; (5) ii. 129–134, fourth encampment.

portion of it, for the material of the main episodes of the poem is drawn chiefly from Exodus xiii. 17–xiv. 31 and Exodus xv. 1–21. It can be seen, therefore, that even less than *Genesis* can this poem properly be called a paraphrase. We shall see later that, in all probability, a very different influence governed its birth. It is indeed an original poem of rare beauty in the sense in which Bright, in this connection, uses the word "original"; that is: "in the sense of being dependent on Scripture for the most part, but independent in the selection and grouping of the material, and artistic in an interweaving of tradition with sacred history, and in observing the demands of a central theme."[1]

Because of this degree of originality in the composition of *Exodus*, and its loose dependence on the Vulgate, the problem of its additional sources has long been of interest. In 1883 Groth[2] suggested that the second division or canto of *Exodus*, which he regarded as an interpolation, was influenced by the poem of Avitus, *De Transitu Maris Rubri*. This view was accepted by Mürkens[3] in his investigation of the sources of *Exodus*. He expresses the opinion also (p. 16) that the Vulgate and the Avitus are the only sources for *Exodus*, and that any expansion of the material so furnished, or additions to it, are to be attributed to the

[1] *Modern Language Notes*, xxvii. 97.
[2] *Composition und Alter der altenglischen angelsächsischen Exodus*, Berlin, 1883, p. 17.
[3] *Untersuchungen über die altenglische Exodus*, Bonn, 1898.

INTRODUCTION liii

refusal of the poetic temperament to be slavishly bound by the material it handles.

This view of the *Exodus* problem was challenged by Samuel Moore in 1911 in a study of the sources of *Exodus*.[1] With admirable thoroughness he re-examines the claims put forward for Avitus as a source. Moore analyses the structure of *Exodus*, and lists fifteen organic additions to the material of the Vulgate—that is, additions which cannot be accounted for as " embellishments or a mere drawing out of the potentialities of the original material," but which " augment it in such a way as to make the work as a whole not only longer, clearer, more interesting, or more beautiful than its source, but essentially different." Two of these fifteen additions [2] Mürkens believed to be drawn from Avitus. Moore is able to show that one of these passages (183-189) contains no proof of dependence upon Avitus whatsoever. The other passage (71-74), which characterizes the pillar of cloud as a protection against heat, has a parallel not only in the *De Transitu*, but also elsewhere in the Scriptures (Num. xiv. 14, Wis. xix. 7, Ps. civ. 39; and St. Jerome's comment upon this passage, *Breviarium in Psalmos*, Migne, xxvi. 1139).[3] It is not necessary, therefore, to postulate dependence upon Avitus in order to explain the presence of this idea in *Exodus*.

[1] " On the Sources of the Old English Exodus," *Modern Philology*, ix. 83-108.

[2] *Exodus*, 71-74 and 183-189.

[3] See also Bright's comments on the eighth " prophecy " for Holy Saturday, in which occurs a similar reference (*Mod. Lang. Notes*, xxvii. 100).

e

INTRODUCTION

Having considered these two instances of organic addition, Moore then takes up eight parallel passages, or instances of similar phraseology, cited by Mürkens as further evidence in support of the theory of Avitus' influence upon *Exodus*. Of these instances only three are found by Moore to have any weight, and in regard to each of them he is able to show superior probability for a belief that the poet of *Exodus* drew from another source than Avitus, or was making a merely natural poetic development of the material already before him.

In 1912 appeared Bright's interesting study of the relations of *Exodus* to the liturgy,[1] a study which suggests a definite unity behind the episodic structure of the poem and, in so doing, goes far toward establishing the much-mooted passage, *Exodus* 362–446, by some critics considered an interpolation, as an integral portion of the poem.[2] Bright maintains the thesis that *Exodus* is " definitely related to the liturgy; that it is specifically ecclesiastic, having been composed in the church,

---

[1] " The Relation of the Cædmonian Exodus to the Liturgy," *Mod. Lang. Notes*, xxvii. 97-103.

[2] As a result of a careful study of the metre of *Exodus* (*Metrik der sogenannten Caedmonschen Dichtungen mit Berücksichtigung der Verfasserfrage*, Weimar, 1894) Graz came to the opinion that lines 362–446 were an interpolation by a later author, but regarded the rest of the poem as the work of a single hand. So also Balg and others. On the other hand, as early as 1882 Ebert (*Anglia*, v. 409–410) protested against the easy rejection of these lines as an interpolation, and gives an interpretation of this passage, and an analysis of its relation to the preceding lines, *cuðe æghwilc mægburga riht, swa him Moses bead, eorla æðelo*, which is in essential agreement with the theory which Bright advances in the article under discussion.

so to speak, as an echo of the service of one of the most elaborate solemnities of the Christian year."[1] The service referred to is that for Holy Saturday, and it is Bright's opinion that the Scriptures or "prophecies" appointed for reading at that service governed the structure of the poem.

The ceremonies of Holy Saturday in the mediæval Church were devoted to the baptism of the catechumens. For them the service was one of much solemnity and rich in symbolism intended to emphasize the meaning of baptism as a spiritual rebirth. The ritual included the reading of twelve "prophecies" or selections from the Scriptures so chosen as to include, with other matter, the stories of the Flood and the Crossing of the Red Sea, legends which had become in the mediæval Church accepted symbolic types of baptism. In these "prophecies" was included also the story of the three youths and the fiery furnace of Daniel, a legend inculcating the glory of martyrdom as a possibility in the Christian warfare in which they were enlisting by baptism. The thesis which Bright upholds is, briefly, that themes present in these various "prophecies" were interwoven by the kindled imagination of the ecclesiastical poet to produce the structural unity of *Exodus*.[2]

Of the twelve "prophecies" two demand particular mention here. The third "prophecy,"

---

[1] *Mod. Lang. Notes*, xxvii. p. 97.

[2] I cannot hope to do justice to Prof. Bright's interesting study in the brief outline possible here. It should be carefully consulted.

Genesis xxii., tells the story of the sacrifice of Isaac. In *Exodus*, 362-446, the poet traces the line of descent from Noah to Abraham, two figures important in relation to the covenant of Israel, a covenant begun with Noah and strengthened by the trial of Abraham. This " prophecy," then, according to Bright's view, may have suggested the theme of lines 362-446 of *Exodus*, and the narrative of the sacrifice of Isaac in *Exodus* represents, not an unmotivated interpolation, but, in a way, indeed, the central theme around which the poem has developed in the poet's mind. In the words of Bright, " Abraham became the father of the nation (*him wæs an fæder*, 353), and to him were made the promises that sustained the national mind. The faith of Abraham, and the destiny of his seed, govern the plan of the poem."

The twelfth " prophecy " consists of the Vulgate Daniel iii. 1-24, containing the legend of the three youths and the fiery furnace. Because of the subject-matter of this last " prophecy," and the fact that the *Daniel* follows immediately after the *Exodus* in the Junius manuscript, Bright seems tempted to find in this " prophecy " the genesis of the Anglo-Saxon *Daniel,* and to assume that both poems are by the same author. " The presumption that has now been established," he says, " in favour of accepting the second composition as the work of the poet of the *Exodus* is, in my judgment, convertible into conviction." This conclusion does not seem fairly based on the slight evidence before us ; it leaves great differences of style in the two

INTRODUCTION

poems still to be accounted for, and apparently disregards all evidence of difference in date. In the case of the *Exodus* it does seem likely that the liturgy afforded a unifying influence governing the introduction of the various *motifs* of that poem. But that the same argument can be extended to the *Daniel* is not apparent.

In any case, Bright's study of the liturgical relations of *Exodus* has thrown new light upon one of the noblest poems of Anglo-Saxon Christian poetry. It is interesting to have had pointed out for us the probability of liturgical influence in the composition of this poem, the same influence that exerted so powerful a moulding pressure upon Cynewulf's *Christ*. The close relation of that poem to the liturgy, most evident in the dependence of Part I. upon the Greater Antiphons of Advent, though manifest throughout, affords a striking instance of strong liturgical influence. If, now, we can with some degree of surety join the *Exodus* with the *Christ* as owing the very unity of its structure to this same relationship, it may indeed be, as Bright suggests, that "Anglo-Saxon poetry as a whole stands in closer relation to the liturgy than has been assumed hitherto," and that early epic and lyric poetry owed more than we have thought to the same influence that was later to play so important a part in the development of early drama.

If style be the criterion, *Exodus* must be judged as of separate and distinct authorship from *Genesis* or *Daniel*. There is in it neither the simplicity of *Genesis A* nor the ordered and restrained narrative of *Daniel*. This poem is marked by a conscious striving for effect; details of description are carefully massed; its compact style abounds in vigorous and unusual imagery. Though *Exodus* may owe its unity of structure to the suggestions of the liturgy, it is in no sense a liturgical poem. Composed as an " echo of the church service " it may have been, but it is an echo that is repeated in the outer world in the light of the sun and the stars and beside great waters. It has often been noticed that the martial scenes of *Exodus* are pictured with so vivid a pen, and characterized by so strong an implication of personal experience, that it is impossible not to believe that at some time in his life the poet had " drunk delight of battle with his peers." Though no battle occurs in *Exodus*, the poet has managed so vividly to create the atmosphere of war in the march of armed men, that from moment to moment we expect the shock of conflict: " Then the hearts of the earls were hopeless within them as they beheld the shining bands, the hosts of Pharaoh, marching from out the south, uplifting a forest of lances, with banners waving above them, a great host treading the border paths. Their spears were in array; shields gleamed and trumpets sang. Over dead bodies circling screamed the birds of battle, dewy-feathered, greedy for war, dark carrion-lovers. In hope of food the wolves, remorseless beasts of slaughter, sang a grim evening song " (154–167). The poet is at home in the camp. He feels a reminiscent joy in mere details of armour, in the trumpet call and the swinging march of a great multitude. The trivial things of experience that stamp themselves upon the memory of men, and spring to mind when the thoughts turn back to some event of sudden triumph or catastrophe, gleam here and there in the lines of *Exodus*. "War-shields flashed. The wall of water, the mighty sea-stream, rushed over the heroes." The vividness of that last flash of sunlight upon armour before the waters closed over the warriors is not the creation of a cloistered imagination. With fierce intensity and poignancy of contrast the poet has symbolized the passionate leap of the heart toward life and the sunlight, in the face of sudden, inevitable doom.

This epic song moves with a steady march which is nowhere checked save in lines 362-446, already considered. The suggestion that this passage owes its presence in the poem to the influence of the liturgy we have already discussed. But it must be confessed that, though these lines are bound into the inner spiritual unity of the poem, they do nevertheless halt the splendid, swinging progress of the descriptive scenes. We feel the poet's imagination turning back from the visualization of the outer world of men and great achievement to a consideration of such things as "the writings tell us."

All that the imagination of this poet pictures it pictures vividly. When the waves of the Red Sea are rolled back, the sight of ocean-bottoms never before uncovered since the beginning of the world is to him as the wonder of a new creation, " the glory and the freshness of a dream." "The ways are dry: grey army-roads, ancient foundations (never have I heard in all the world that men before set foot thereon), shining plains, imprisoned deep sea-bottoms, over which of old the great waves foamed." The waters are erected into ramparts by the might of God, and, when God wills, these ramparts crumble, and the sea falls upon the Egyptians. "Fate cut off retreat, and locked them in the sea."

The true underlying theme of *Exodus*, as of all this cycle, is the power and glory of God, who putteth down the mighty from their seats. Over and over in the Junius poems, as an epilogue to tales of swift and tragic catastrophe, are heard, as here, the words of the poet: "For they had striven against God." In the concluding lines of *Exodus* the last thought is of God's might. For the eyes of the poet look beyond the rejoicing multitude upon the sea-shore gathering the spoils of the foe, to the dark waters where "the greatest of armies lay still in that place of death."

DANIEL

The *Daniel*, a poem of 765 lines, immediately following the *Exodus*, comprises sections 50–55 of Part I. of the Junius manuscript. The poem is broken off by a defect in the manuscript, leaving the account of Belshazzar's Feast incomplete. The introductory lines of the poem deal with the prosperity of the Jews in Jerusalem and their resultant arrogance and disobedience. There follows an account of the capture of the city by Nebuchadnezzar, the selection of youths for public training, the king's first dream and Daniel's interpretation of it, the setting up of the golden image and the decree of worship, the refusal of the three youths to worship and their miraculous fate in the fiery furnace, the king's dream of the tree and Daniel's interpretation of it, the exile and return of Nebuchadnezzar, and a partial account of Belshazzar's Feast. The main episodes of the poem are based upon the Vulgate version of Daniel i.-v. The source is followed with some closeness, and the addition of little extraneous matter, in which respect *Daniel* differs widely from the *Exodus*. The introductory lines are not based upon the Vulgate, and the reference in these introductory lines to the departure of the Israelites from Egypt affords opportunity for interesting conjecture regarding the relation of *Daniel* to *Exodus*. It is possible that these introductory lines were composed by the compiler of Part I. of the Junius manuscript as a transitional link between *Exodus* and *Daniel*.

Lines 283-332 of *Daniel*, comprising the "Prayer of Azariah," and 362-408, the "Song of the Three Youths," with their connective narrative matter, correspond to a poem in the Exeter Book, the so-called *Azarias*. The first of these two lyrics, *Daniel*, 279-361, corresponds so closely to the first 75 lines of the *Azarias* that we are forced to regard them as variant versions of the same poem. One view of the relation of these two poems assigns priority of date to *Azarias*, and regards it as the original of this part of *Daniel*. Such evidence as can be found in support of this view has been obtained by the usual metre and grammar tests. It is by no means conclusive, however, and it may be that both in this section of *Daniel* and in the *Azarias* we have revisions of an older poem. Facts are not at hand to determine this question beyond dispute.¹ The lyric passage of lines 362–408 of *Daniel* is based not upon the Vulgate, but upon a version of the *Cantus trium puerorum*, preserved among the Vespasian Hymns.² This dependence is evidenced by a number of correspondences between *Daniel* and the Vespasian Hymn at points where both are at variance with the Vulgate. The influence of the hymn may well have been due to its use as a canticle in the church services.

It may be questioned whether *Daniel* has usually been ranked as high by the critics as it deserves on

¹ Hofer in his study of the structure of *Daniel* ("Über die Entstehung des Angelsächsischen Gedichtes Daniel," *Anglia*, xii. 158–204) expresses the view that the author did not intend, when he began his composition of *Daniel*, to do more than treat the fate of the three youths in the fiery furnace, definitely concluding the poem with verses 278–279: "That was the God of glory who preserved them from that peril." Later, however, according to Hofer's conjecture, the author became acquainted with an *Azarias* poem, of which the *Azarias* of the Exeter Book is a variant. Appreciating its beauty. the author added these lines to the portion of *Daniel* already composed, not noticing certain repetitions caused by this union, or regarding them as unimportant, and then devoted himself in lines 410 ff. to a versification of the remaining episodes of *Daniel*.

² See Steiner, *Über die Interpolation im angelsächsischen Gedichte Daniel*, Leipzig, 1889.

grounds of poetic merit. It has been called a "dreary poem," and is often passed over with brief comment. Very possibly the position of *Daniel* in the Junius manuscript, and the comparison with *Exodus* which that position makes almost inevitable, is responsible for this. No comparison could be less fortunate. The *Exodus* is an epic song marked by vivid imagination, unusual descriptive power, and poetic imagery. The *Daniel* is an episodic narrative poem of the type of *Genesis A*. The narrative shows a considerable degree of skill, giving the impression of orderly choice of material and a restrained, but none the less real, poetic power. Now and again, as in the conversion of Nebuchadnezzar, the verse attains nobility, and the style is free from that breathless rush which is half a merit and half a fault in *Exodus*. The setting up of the golden image, the refusal of the youths to worship, and the miracle of the fiery furnace, are vividly described, here and there a detail calling to our minds the martyrdom of Cynewulf's *Juliana*. And in the Prayer of Azariah and the Song of the Three Youths we have passages in which the lyric note of the original is adequately reproduced. In *Daniel*, as has been often noted, occurs one of the few similes found in Anglo-Saxon poetry, and one of the most beautiful, a simile found twice again in the poem in slightly altered form : " No whit of harm had come to them, but within the furnace it was just as when in the summer season the sun shineth and the dew-fall cometh at dawn, scattered by the wind."

INTRODUCTION

It must be admitted that the episode of Belshazzar's feast displays no great evidence of poetic skill. It is incomplete because of a defect in the manuscript, but in the portion that has remained to us we have a narrative of slight merit. That part of *Daniel*, however, which describes Nebuchadnezzar's dream of the tree, Daniel's interpretation of that dream, and the metamorphosis of Nebuchadnezzar, rises to the height of its great theme more fully perhaps than any other portion of the poem. The description of the dream itself has a poetic beauty which is enhanced by the restraint of the style. And surely nowhere in Anglo-Saxon poetry is there a more simple or intimate expression of faith than in the passage in which the poet describes the coming of belief to the humbled heart of the king: " Then the wretched man, companion of the beasts, looked up through the flying clouds, and he knew in his heart that there was a Lord and King of heaven, and one Eternal Spirit ruling over the sons of men. And he was recovered from the madness which long had been upon him, vexing the heart and soul of the king."

CHRIST AND SATAN

Christ and Satan, a poem of 733 lines, divided into 12 sections, comprises the second part of the Junius manuscript. It falls into three divisions which have been distinguished and named as follows: lines 1–365, *The Lament of the Fallen Angels*; lines 366–664, *The Harrowing of Hell*; lines 665–733,

INTRODUCTION lxv

The Temptation. Groschopp[1] attempted to show that in *Christ and Satan* we are dealing with fragments of a single longer original which a later scribe had attempted to restore to unity by poetic links of his own invention. Ten Brink[2] and Wülker[3] regarded *Christ and Satan* as a union of three separate poems. Brandl,[4] however, finds elements of unity in the three divisions, and a recent critic, Frings,[5] is strongly of the view that no case has been made out against the unity of the poem. Groschopp regarded the poem, basing his opinion on characteristics of the language, as older than the other poems of the Junius manuscript. This view has been generally rejected. Scholars, on the whole, agree in dating the *Christ and Satan* a little later than the work of Cynewulf.[6]

The first division of the poem, or *The Lament of the Fallen Angels*, represents Satan and his fellows as bewailing their sin in hell, and dreading God's further vengeance. The description of hell itself is far more vigorously wrought out than in *Genesis B*. The Teutonic elements which we noticed in the hell of *Genesis B* are present in *The Lament of the Fallen Angels*, with the addition of a number of details,

---

[1] *Das Angelsächsische Gedicht " Crist und Satan,"* Halle, 1883.
[2] *English Literature*, i. 86.   [3] *Grundriss*, 131, note.
[4] *Geschichte der Altenglischen Literatur*, 1045–1046.
[5] " Christ und Satan," T. Frings, *Zeitschrift für deutsche Philologie*, xlv. 217–236, 1913–1914.
[6] See Brandl, *Geschichte der Altenglischen Literatur*, 1908; A. J. Barnouw, *Textkritische Untersuchungen*, Leiden, 1902; Carl Richter, "Chronologische Studien zur Angelsächsischen Literatur," *Studien zur Englischen Philologie*, xxxiii. 1910.

clear and definite, which appear here only. Hell is pictured as a windy hall, in the lowest abyss; its floors burn with fire and venom; its gates are guarded by dragons. Through its wide and dreary spaces resounds the woe and anguish of the accursed. "They have no hope but only frost and fire, torture and pain and swarming serpents, dragons and adders and a house of darkness. He who stood within twelve miles of hell might hear a gnashing of teeth, loud and full of woe."

In this grim hall Satan in his bondage confesses his former sin in heaven. We have no longer the sure, defiant voice of *Genesis B*. A note of realization of sin and the wages of sin is struck again and again in the speeches of Satan. Though his words "fly forth like sparks," we know that this voice could not utter that broken threat of vengeance which the Satan of *Genesis B*, fast in hell's bondage, hurls against God. It is part of the punishment of Satan that over and over he must rehearse his sin and the beauty of the heavenly life which, through that sin, has passed from him for ever, even as Marlowe makes Mephistopheles cry:

> "Think'st thou that I who saw the face of God,
> And tasted the eternal joys of Heaven,
> Am not tormented with ten thousand hells,
> In being deprived of everlasting bliss?"

Gone, too, are his power and dominion over the fallen angels. The Satan of *Genesis B* still retained his sovereignty. But in this poem Satan is scorned and cursed by those that fell with him, and ever as

INTRODUCTION lxvii

an antiphonal to his confessions come their taunts:
"Loathsome is thy face! Sorely have we suffered
for thy lies!"

The Harrowing of Hell is based upon the second
part of the apocryphal *Gospel of Nicodemus*. This
story of the Passion, Resurrection, and Descent of
Christ arose probably in the fourth century and
became exceedingly popular during the Middle
Ages. Becoming known to the early Latin writers
of England, it has survived in three Old English
prose versions and furnishes the *motif* for somewhat
extended treatment in three separate Anglo-Saxon
poems.[1] The theme of Christ's descent into hell
receives the same general development in *Christ
and Satan* and in the *Harrowing of Hell* of the
Exeter Book. Cynewulf's *Christ* (Part II.) contains
a brief lyric treatment of the same theme.[2]

In the poem before us a short introduction
describes the revolt of Satan and his banishment
to hell. Then swiftly follows the coming of the
Judge. "Before Him shineth a fairer light than
ever our eyes beheld save when we dwelt among
the angels." There is thunder in the dawn. God
has come to overthrow the powers of hell and redeem thence the souls of the chosen. Eve's voice,
silent since *Genesis*, is heard once more, re-telling
the sin of Eden, and beseeching mercy of God for
Mary's sake, daughter of Eve. Then the Eternal

---

[1] W. H. Hulme, "The Old English Gospel of Nicodemus,"
Modern Language Ass. Publications, xiii. 457–542, and *Modern
Philology*, i. 579–614.

[2] *Christ*, 558–585.

lxviii   INTRODUCTION

Lord thrusts the fiends " deeper into that deep darkness," and leads the blessed unto their native home in heaven. From the conclusion of the *Harrowing of Hell* episode to the end of this second division the verse falls into a number of short sections dealing with the Resurrection, Ascension, and Last Judgment, so that this second division of *Christ and Satan* may represent a number of shorter poems here united by the scribe.

The third division of the poem is a broken fragment of *The Temptation*, noteworthy only in one passage, but in that preserving for us one of the finest bits of noble verse in the Junius manuscript—that in which Christ sends Satan back to measure hell's torment that he may realize God's might. " Know, accursed Fiend, how measureless and wide and dreary is the pit of hell! Measure it with thy hands, take hold upon its bottom! Go then until thou knowest all the circle of it. Measure it first from above even unto the abyss. Measure how broad the black mist stretches! Then shalt thou know more clearly that thou strivest against God."

So ends the Junius manuscript. There is an objective reality in the Junian poems that carries conviction to the heart when greater art may fail. The wistful, tender cadences of Cynewulf, his expression of personal weakness, and penitence, and aspiration have no parallel in these poems. In them the poet loses himself in the greatness of the visions that float before his dreaming eyes. Even the loveliness of nature is objectively described.

Cynewulf's sense of the beauty of the world is increased by his realization that life is transient, evanescent. His joy in a thousand moods of landscape and sea is made wistful by the thought that this loveliness must fade. But it is a childlike and self-forgetful simplicity that paints the natural scenes in the Junian poems, the morning beauty of a new-made world, fresh from the hand of the Creator, the sunlight and divided seas of *Exodus*, the rain and flying clouds of Nebuchadnezzar's exile.

The characterization of the chief actors in these poems is successful in the same way, and through the same qualities. Though often very simply drawn, with a few swift strokes, the drawing is sure and firm, and the figures that move through the pages of the Junian manuscript are filled with the breath of life. Eve is a really great figure, more consistent, more appealing, than the Eve of *Paradise Lost*. Satan, surrounded by his followers, as in *Genesis*, or forsaken and flouted as in *Christ and Satan*, is a magnificent and terrible conception.

It is indeed the strong and vivid personalization of the powers of good and evil, as protagonists in a universal drama, which produces the majesty and grandeur of the Junian poems. They portray a warfare, expressed in terms of Christian faith, between the powers of light and the powers of darkness, beginning with the titanic struggle between God and Lucifer which results in the temptation and fall of man, and ending with the conquest of the hosts of evil in the *Harrowing of Hell*.

f

There is a sublimity of theme in *Genesis* and a magnificence of conception in parts of *Christ and Satan* that make them, in a way, incommensurable with other Anglo-Saxon religious poems. The great drama unfolds in universal space, through infinite time. Amid the thunder of an elemental struggle man's life is born upon the green earth. The powers of evil for a moment prevail; the sky darkens, and man goes forth to exile. The innocent loveliness of the world fades slowly to the light of common day. Yet by love, divine and sacrificial, eternity is reclaimed, and Satan bound for ever. " So shalt thou know more clearly that thou strivest against God."

It is no shadowy conception of the divine that is realized in the Junian poems, but a God of almighty power and infinite love, of justice and mercy. An abiding sense of God's covenant with His people binds into unity these tales of His loving guidance or stern correction. Through all the changing pattern of tragic doom and catastrophe, of heroic deed and sacrificial faith, interwoven as an unbroken thread, runs the divine purpose. It is the portrayal of this divine purpose that is the great and central theme of these poems, artlessly wrought in simple sincerity, and clothed with the light of transcendent truth—a poet's vision

> " Upon the great world's altar-stairs
> That slope through darkness up to God."

CÆDMON'S HYMN

A

THE CÆDMON POEMS

CÆDMON'S HYMN

PRAISE we the Lord
Of the heavenly kingdom,
God's power and wisdom,
The works of His hand ;
As the Father of glory,
Eternal Lord,
Wrought the beginning
Of all His wonders !
Holy Creator !
Warden of men !
First, for a roof,
O'er the children of earth,
He stablished the heavens,
And founded the world,
And spread the dry land
For the living to dwell in.
Lord Everlasting !
Almighty God !

GENESIS

GENESIS

RIGHT is it that we praise the King of heaven, the Lord of hosts, and love Him with all our hearts. For He is great in power, the Source of all created things, the Lord Almighty. Never hath He known beginning, neither cometh an end of His eternal glory. Ever in majesty He reigneth over celestial thrones; in righteousness and strength He keepeth the courts of heaven which were established, broad and ample, by the might of God, for angel dwellers, wardens of the soul. The angel legions knew the blessedness of God, celestial joy and bliss. Great was their glory! The mighty spirits magnified their Prince and sang His praise with gladness, serving the Lord of life, exceeding blessed in His splendour. They knew no sin nor any evil; but dwelt in peace for ever with their Lord. They wrought no deed in heaven save right and truth, until the angel prince in pride walked in the ways of error. Then no longer would they work their own advantage, but turned away from the love of God. They boasted greatly, in their banded strength, that they could share with God His glorious dwelling, spacious and heavenly bright.

Then sorrow came upon them, envy and insolence and pride of the angel who first began that deed of folly, to plot and hatch it forth, and, thirsting for battle, boasted that in the northern borders of heaven he would stablish a throne and a kingdom. Then was God angered and wrathful against that host which He had crowned before with radiance and glory. For the traitors, to reward their work, He shaped a house of pain and grim affliction, and lamentations of hell. Our Lord prepared this torture-house of exiles, deep and joyless, for the coming of the angel hosts. Well He knew it lay enshrouded in eternal night, and filled with woe, wrapped in fire and piercing cold, smoke-veils and ruddy flame. And over that wretched realm He spread the brooding terror of torment. They had wrought grievous wrong together against God. Grim the reward they gained!

Fierce of heart, they boasted they would take the kingdom, and easily. But their hope failed them when the Lord, High King of heaven, lifted His hand against their host. The erring spirits, in their sin, might not prevail against the Lord, but God, the Mighty, in His wrath, smote their insolence and broke their pride, bereft these impious souls of victory and power and dominion and glory; despoiled His foes of bliss and peace and joy and radiant grace, and mightily avenged His wrath upon them to their destruction. His heart was hardened against them; with heavy hand He crushed His foes, subdued them to His will, and, in His wrath, drove out the rebels from their ancient home and seats of glory. Our Lord expelled and banished out of heaven the presumptuous angel host. All-wielding God dismissed the faithless horde, a hostile band of woeful spirits, upon a long, long journey. Crushed was their pride, their boasting humbled, their power broken, their glory dimmed. Thenceforth those dusky spirits dwelt in exile. No cause had they to laugh aloud, but, racked with pangs of hell, they suffered pain and woe and tribulation, cloaked with darkness, knowing bitter anguish, a grim requital, because they sought to strive with God.

Then was there calm as formerly in heaven, the kindly ways of peace. The Lord was dear to all, a Prince among His thanes, and glory was renewed of angel legions knowing blessedness with God. The citizens of heaven, the home of glory, dwelt again in concord. Strife was at an end among the angels, discord and dissension, when those warring spirits, shorn of light, were hurled from heaven. Behind them stretching wide their mansions lay, crowned with glory, prospering in grace in God's dominion, a sunny, fruitful land. empty of dwellers,

58-89

when the accursed spirits reached their place of exile within Hell's prison-walls.

Then our Lord took counsel in the thoughts of His heart how He might people, with a better host, the great creation, the native seats and gleaming mansions, high in heaven, wherefrom these boastful foes had got them forth. Therefore with mighty power Holy God ordained, beneath the arching heavens, that earth and sky and the far-bounded sea should be established, earth-creatures in the stead of those rebellious foes whom He had cast from heaven.

As yet was nought save shadows of darkness; the spacious earth lay hidden, deep and dim, alien to God, unpeopled and unused. Thereon the Steadfast King looked down and beheld it, a place empty of joy. He saw dim chaos hanging in eternal night, obscure beneath the heavens, desolate and dark, until this world was fashioned by the word of the King of glory. Here first with mighty power the Everlasting Lord, the Helm of all created things, Almighty King, made earth and heaven, raised up the sky and founded the spacious land. The earth was not yet green with grass; the dark waves of the sea flowed over it, and midnight darkness was upon it, far and wide.

Then in radiant glory God's holy spirit moved upon the waters with wondrous might. The Lord of angels, Giver of life, bade

light shine forth upon the spacious earth.
Swiftly was God's word fulfilled; holy light
gleamed forth across the waste at the
Creator's bidding. Over the seas the Lord
of victory divided light from darkness,
shadow from radiant light. The Lord of
life gave both a name. By the word of God
the gleaming light was first called day. And
in the beginning of creation was God well
pleased. The first day saw the dark and
brooding shadows vanish throughout the
spacious earth.

The day departed, hasting over the dwellings of earth. And after the gleaming light
the Lord, our Maker, thrust on the first of
evenings. Murky gloom pressed hard upon
the heels of day; God called it night. Our
Lord sundered them, one from the other;
and ever since they follow out the will of
God to do it on the earth.

Then came a second day, light after darkness. And the Lord of life ordained a
pleasant firmament amid the waters. Our
Lord sundered the seas and established the
heavens. By His word the King, Almighty
God, raised them above the earth. The
waters were divided under the heavens by
His holy might; the waters were sundered
from the waters, under the firmament.

Then came hasting over the earth the third
fair morning. Not yet were the wide ways
and spacious tracts useful unto God, but the

land lay covered by the deep. The Lord of angels, by His word, commanded that the waters come together, which now beneath the heavens hold their course and place ordained. Then suddenly, wide-stretching under heaven, lay the sea, as God gave bidding. The great deep was sundered from the land. The Warden of life, the Lord of hosts, beheld the dry ground far outspread. And the King of glory called it earth. For the ocean-billows and the wide-flung sea He set a lawful path and fettered them. . . .

It did not seem good to the Lord of heaven that Adam should longer be alone as warden and keeper of this new Paradise. Wherefore the King, Almighty God, wrought him an helpmeet; the Author of life made woman and brought her unto the man whom He loved. He took the stuff of Adam's body, and secretly drew forth a rib from his side. He was fast asleep in peaceful slumber; he knew no pain nor any pang; there came no blood from out the wound, but the Lord of angels drew forth from his body a growing rib, and the man was unhurt. Of this God fashioned a lovely maid, breathing into her life and an eternal soul. They were like unto the angels. The bride of Adam . . . was a living spirit. By God's might both were born into the world in the loveliness of youth. They knew no sin nor any evil, but in the hearts of both there burned the love of God.

Then the Gracious King, Lord of all human kind, blessed these two, male and female, man and wife, and spake this word:

"Be fruitful and multiply, and fill the green earth with your seed and increase, sons and daughters. And ye shall have dominion over the salt sea, and over all the world. Enjoy the riches of earth, the fish of the sea, and the fowls of the air. To you is given power over the herds which I have hallowed, and the wild beasts, and over all living things that move upon the earth; all living things, which the depths bring forth throughout the sea, shall be subject unto you."

And our Lord beheld the beauty of His works and the abundance of all fruits of this new creation: Paradise lay pleasant and inviting, filled with goodly store and endless blessings. Bountifully a running stream, a welling spring, watered that pleasant land. Not yet did clouds, dark with wind, carry the rains across the spacious earth; nathless the land lay decked with increase. Out from this new Paradise four pleasant brooks of water flowed. All were divisions of one beauteous stream, sundered by the might of God when He made the earth, and sent into the world. And one of these the mortal dwellers of earth called Pison, which compasseth the land of Havilah about with shining waters. And in that land, as books tell us, the sons of men from far and near find out the best of gold and precious gems. And the second floweth round about the land and borders of the Ethiopians, a spacious kingdom. Its name is Gihon. The third is Tigris, whose abundant stream lieth about the limits of Assyria. Likewise also the fourth, which now through many a folk-land men call Euphrates. . . .

(Beginning of Genesis B)

"Eat freely of the fruit of every other tree. From that one tree refrain. Beware of its fruit. And ye shall know no dearth of pleasant things."

Eagerly they bowed them down before the King of heaven, and gave Him thanks for all, for His teachings and counsels. And He gave them that land to dwell in. Then the Holy Lord, the Steadfast King, departed into heaven. And the creatures of His hand abode together on the earth. They had no whit of care to grieve them, but only to do the will of God for ever. Dear were they unto God as long as they would keep His holy word.

The Holy Lord, All-wielding God, with mighty hand had wrought ten angel-orders in whom He trusted well, that they would do Him service, and work His will. Therefore God gave them reason, with His own hands shaped them, and stablished them in bliss. But one He made so great and strong of heart, He let him wield such power in heaven next unto God, so radiant-hued He wrought him, so fair his form in heaven which God had given, that he was like unto the shining stars. He should have sung his Maker's praise, and prized his bliss in heaven. He should have thanked his Lord for the great boon He showered on him in the heavenly light, and let him long enjoy. But he turned him to a worse thing, and strove to stir up strife against the Highest Lord of heaven, who sitteth on the throne of glory.

Dear was he to our Lord. Nor could it long be hid from God that pride was growing in His angel's heart. He set himself against his Leader, scoffed at God with boasting, and would not serve Him. He said his form was beautiful and bright, gleaming and fair of hue. Nor could he find it in his heart to serve the Lord God, or be subject to Him. It seemed to him that he had greater strength and larger following than Holy God might have. Many words the angel spake in his presumption. By his own power alone he thought to build a stronger throne and mightier in heaven. He said his heart was urging him to toil, to build a stately palace in the north and west. He said he doubted in his heart if he would still be subject unto God :

"Why should I slave?" quoth he. "I

need not serve a master. My hands are strong to work full many a wonder. Power enough have I to rear a goodlier throne, a higher in the heavens. Why should I fawn for His favour, or yield Him such submission? I may be God as well as He! Brave comrades stand about me; stout-hearted heroes who will not fail me in the fray. These valiant souls have chosen me their lord. With such peers one may ponder counsel, and gain a following. Devoted are these friends and faithful-hearted; and I may be their lord and rule this realm. It seemeth no wise right to me that I should cringe a whit to God for any good. I will not serve Him longer."

Now when God had heard all this, how His angel was beginning to make presumptuous head against his Leader, speaking rash words of insolence against his Lord, needs must he make atonement for that deed, endure the woe of strife, and bear his punishment, most grievous of all deaths. And so doth every man who wickedly thinketh to strive with God, the Lord of might.

Then Almighty God, High Lord of heaven, was filled with wrath, and hurled him from his lofty throne. He had gained his Master's hate, and lost His favour. God's heart was hardened against him. Wherefore he needs must sink into the pit of torment because he strove against the Lord of heaven. He banished him from grace and cast him into hell, into the deep abyss where he became a devil. The Fiend and all his followers fell from heaven; three nights and days the angels fell from heaven into hell. God changed them all to devils. Because they heeded not His deed and word, therefore Almighty God hurled them into darkness, deep under earth, crushed them and set them in the mirk of hell. There through the never-ending watches of the night the fiends endure an unremitting fire. Then at the dawn cometh an east wind, and bitter frost, ever a blast of fire or storm of frost. And each must have his share of suffering wrought for his punishment. Their world was changed when God filled full the pit of hell with His foes!

But the angels who kept their faith with God dwelt in the heights of heaven. The other fiends who waged so fierce a war with God lay wrapped in flames. They suffer torment, hot and surging flame in the midst of hell, broad-stretching blaze of fire and bitter smoke, darkness and gloom, because they broke allegiance unto God. Their folly and the angel's pride deceived them. They would not heed the word of God. Great was their punishment! They fell, through folly and through pride, to fiery depths of flame in hell. They sought another home devoid of light and filled with fire—a mighty flaming death. The fiends perceived that through the might of God, because of their presumptuous hearts and boundless insolence, they had won a measureless woe.

Then spake their haughty king, who formerly was fairest of the angels, most radiant in heaven, beloved of his Leader and dear unto his Lord, until they turned to folly, and Almighty God was moved to anger at their wantonness, and hurled him down to depths of torment on that bed of death. He named him with a name, and said their leader should be called from thenceforth Satan. He bade him rule the black abyss of hell in place of striving against God. Satan spake—who now must needs have charge of hell and dwell in the abyss— in bitterness he spake who once had been God's angel, radiant-hued in heaven, until his pride and boundless arrogance betrayed him, so that he would not do the bidding of the Lord of hosts. Bitterness was welling in his heart ; and round him blazed his cruel torment. These words he spake :

"This narrow place is little like those other realms we knew, on high in heaven, allotted by my Lord, though the Almighty hath not granted us to hold our state, or rule our kingdom. He hath done us wrong to hurl us to the fiery depths of hell, and strip us of our heavenly realm. He hath ordained that human kind shall settle there. That is my greatest grief that Adam—wrought of earth—should hold my firm-set throne and live in joy, while we endure this bitter woe in hell.

"Alas! could I but use my hands and have my freedom for an hour, one winter hour, then with this host I would—— But bands of iron crush me down, the bondage of my chains is heavy. I am stripped of my dominion. Firmly are hell's fetters forged upon me. Above me and below a blaze of fire! Never have I seen a realm more fatal—flame unassuaged that surges over hell. Ensnaring links and heavy shackles hold me. My ways are trammelled up; my feet are bound; my hands are fastened. Closed are the doors of hell, the way cut off. I may not escape out of my bonds, but mighty gyves of tempered iron, hammered hot, press hard upon me. God hath set His foot upon my neck. So I know the Lord of hosts hath read the purpose of my heart, and knew full well that strife would grow between our host and Adam over the heavenly realm, had I the freedom of my hands.

"But now we suffer throes of hell, fire and darkness, bottomless and grim. God hath thrust us out into the black mists. He cannot charge upon us any sin or evil wrought against Him in His realm! Yet hath He robbed us of the light and cast us into utter woe. Nor may we take revenge, nor do

Him any evil because He stripped us of the light. He hath marked out the borders of the world, and there created man in His own image, with whom He hopes again to people heaven, with pure souls. We needs must ponder earnestly to wreak this grudge on Adam, if we may, and on his children, and thwart His will if so we may devise.

"No longer have I any hope of light wherein He thinketh long to joy, in bliss among His angel hosts; nor may we ever bring this thing to pass, that we should change the purpose of Almighty God. Let us therefore turn the heavenly kingdom from the sons of men, since we may not possess it, cause them to lose His favour and turn aside from the command He laid upon them. Then shall His wrath be kindled, and He shall cast them out from grace. They shall seek out hell and its grim gulf, and in this heavy bondage we may have the sons of men to serve us.

"Begin now and plan this enterprise. If ever in olden days, when happily we dwelt in that good kingdom, and held possession of our thrones, I dealt out princely treasure to any thane, he could not make requital for my gifts at any better time than now, if some one of my thanes would be my helper, escaping outward through these bolted gates, with strength to wing his way on high where, new-created, Adam and Eve, surrounded with abundance, dwell on earth—and we are cast out hither in this deep abyss. They are now much dearer unto God, and own the high estate and rightful realm which we should have in heaven! Good fortune is allotted to mankind.

"My soul is sorrowful within me, my heart is sore, that they should hold the heavenly realm for ever. But if in any wise some one of you could bring them to forsake God's word and teaching, soon would they be less pleasing unto Him! If they break His commandment, then will His wrath be kindled. Their high estate shall vanish; their sin shall have requital, and some grim penalty. Take thought now how ye may ensnare them. I shall rest softly in these chains if they lose heaven. Whoso shall bring this thing to pass shall have reward for ever, of all that we may win to our advantage, amid these flames. I will let him sit next me, whoever shall return to hell proclaiming that they have set at naught, by word and deed, the counsels of the King of heaven and been displeasing to the Lord." [1]

Then God's enemy began to make him ready, equipped in war-gear, with a wily heart. He set his helm of darkness on his head, bound it full hard, and fastened it with clasps. Many a crafty speech he knew, many a crooked word. Upward he beat his

[1] Grein: *lare forleton and wurdon lað gode.*

way and darted through the doors of hell. He had a ruthless heart. Evil of purpose he circled in the air, cleaving the flame with fiendish craft. He would fain ensnare God's servants unto sin, seduce them and deceive them that they might be displeasing to the Lord. With fiendish craft he took his way until he came on Adam upon earth, the finished handiwork of God, full wisely wrought, and his wife beside him, loveliest of women, performing many a goodly service since the Lord of men appointed them His ministers.

And by them stood two trees laden with fruit and clothed with increase. Almighty God, High King of heaven, had set them there that the mortal sons of men might choose of good and evil, weal and woe. Unlike was their fruit! Of the one tree the fruit was pleasant, fair and winsome, excellent and sweet. That was the tree of life. He might live for ever in the world who ate of that fruit, so that old age pressed not heavily upon him, nor grievous sickness, but he might live his life in happiness for ever, and have the favour of the King of heaven here on earth. And glory was ordained for him in heaven, when he went hence.

The other tree was dark, sunless, and full of shadows: that was the tree of death. Bitter the fruit it bore! And every man must know both good and evil; in this world abased he needs must suffer, in sweat and sorrow, who tasted of the fruit that grew upon that tree. Old age would rob him of his strength and joy and honour, and death take hold upon him. A little time might he enjoy this life, and then seek out the murky realm of flame, and be subject unto fiends. There of all perils are the worst for men for ever. And that the evil one knew well, the wily herald of the fiend who fought with God. He took the form of a serpent, coiled round the tree of death by devil's craft, and plucked the fruit, and turned aside again where he beheld the handiwork of the King of heaven. And the evil one in lying words began to question him:

"Hast thou any longing, Adam, unto God? His service brings me hither from afar. Not long since I was sitting at His side. He sent me forth upon this journey to bid thee eat this fruit. He said thy strength and power would increase, thy mind be mightier, more beautiful thy body, and thy form more fair. He said thou wouldest lack no good thing on the earth when thou hast won the favour of the King of heaven, served thy Lord with gladness, and deserved His love.

"In the heavenly light I heard Him speaking of thy life, praising thy words and works. Needs must thou do His bidding which His messengers proclaim on earth.

Broad-stretching are the green plains of the world, and from the highest realms of heaven God ruleth all things here below. The Lord of men will not Himself endure the hardship to go upon this journey, but sendeth His ministers to speak with thee. He sendeth tidings unto thee to teach thee wisdom. Do His will with gladness! Take this fruit in thy hand; taste and eat. Thy heart shall grow more roomy and thy form more fair. Almighty God, thy Lord, sendeth this help from heaven."

And Adam, first of men, answered where he stood on earth: "When I heard the Lord, my God, speaking with a mighty voice, He bade me dwell here keeping His commandments, gave me this woman, this lovely maid, bade me take heed and be not tempted to the tree of death and utterly beguiled, and said that he who taketh to his heart one whit of evil shall dwell in blackest hell. Though thou art come with lies and secret wiles, I know not that thou art an angel of the Lord from heaven. Lo! I cannot understand thy precepts, thy words or ways, thy errand or thy sayings. I know what things our Lord commanded when I beheld Him nigh at hand. He bade me heed His word, observe it well, and keep His precepts. Thou art not like to any of His angels that ever I have seen, nor hast thou showed me any token that my Lord hath sent of grace and favour. Therefore I cannot hearken to thy teachings. Get thee hence! I have my faith set firm upon Almighty God, who with His own hands wrought me. From His high throne He giveth all good things, and needeth not to send His ministers."

Then turned the fiend with wrathful heart to where he saw Eve standing on the plains of earth, a winsome maid. And unto her he said, the greatest of all ills thereafter would fall on their descendants in the world:

"I know God's anger will be roused against you, when from this journey through far-stretching space I come again to Him, and bring this message, that ye refuse to do His bidding, as He hath sent commandment hither from the East. He needs must come to speak with you, forsooth, nor may His minister proclaim His mission! Truly I know His wrath will be kindled against you in His heart!

"But if thou, woman, wilt hearken to my words, thou mayest devise good counsel. Bethink thee in thy heart to turn away His vengeance from you both, as I shall show thee. Eat of this fruit! Then shall thine eyes grow keen, and thou shalt see afar through all the world, yea! unto the throne of God, thy Lord, and have His favour. Thou mayest rule the heart of Adam, if thou incline to do it and he doth trust thy words, if thou wilt tell him truly what law thou hast in mind, to keep God's precepts and commandments. His heart will cease from bitter strife and evil answers, as we two tell him for his good. Urge him earnestly to do thy bidding, lest ye be displeasing to the Lord your God. If thou fulfill this undertaking, thou best of women, I will not tell our Lord what evil Adam spake against me, his wicked words accusing me of falsehood, saying that I am eager in transgression, a servant of the Fiend and not God's angel. But I know well the angel race, and the high courts of heaven. Long ages have I served the Lord my God with loyal heart. I am not like a devil."

So he urged with lies and luring wiles, tempting the woman unto sin, until the serpent's counsel worked within her—for God had wrought her soul the weaker—and her heart inclined according to his teaching. Transgressing God's commandment, from the fiend she took the fatal fruit of the tree of death. Never was worse deed wrought for men! Great is the wonder that Eternal God, the Lord, would let so many of His thanes be tricked with lies by one who brought such counsel. She ate the fruit and set at naught the will and word of God.

Then could she see afar by gift of the fiend, whose lies deceived and artfully ensnared her, so that it came to pass the heavens appeared to her more radiant, and the earth and all the world more fair, the great and mighty handiwork of God, though she beheld it not by human wisdom; but eagerly the fiend deceived her soul and gave her vision, that she might see afar across the heavenly kingdom. Then spake the fiend with hostile purpose — and nought of profit did he counsel:

"Now mayest thou behold, most worthy Eve, nor need I tell thee, how fair thy beauty and thy form how changed, since thou didst trust my words and do my bidding. A radiance shineth round about thee, gleaming splendour, which I brought forth from God on high. Thou mayest touch it! Tell Adam what vision thou hast and power by my coming. And even yet, if he will do my bidding with humble heart, I will give him of this light abundantly, as I have given thee, and will not punish his reviling words, though he deserves no mercy for the grievous ill he spake against me. So shall his children live hereafter! When they do evil, they must win God's love, avert His doom, and gain the favour of their Lord for ever!"

Then the lovely maid, fairest of women that ever came into this world, went unto Adam. She was the handiwork of the King of heaven, though tricked with lies and utterly undone, so that through fiendish craft and devil's fraud she needs must be displeasing to the Lord, forfeit God's favour, and lose her glory and her heavenly home.

605–633

So often evil dwelleth with that man who doth not shun it when he hath the power.

Of the fatal apples some she carried in her hands and some lay on her breast, the fruit of the tree of death whereof the Lord of lords, the Prince of glory, had forbidden her to eat, saying His servants need not suffer death. The Holy Lord bestowed a heavenly heritage and ample bliss on every race, if they would but forgo that fruit alone, that bitter fruit, which the mortal tree brought forth upon its boughs. That was the tree of death which the Lord forbade them!

But the fiend, who hated God, and loathed the King of heaven, deceived with lies Eve's heart and erring wisdom, and she believed his words and did his bidding, and came at last to think his counsels were indeed from God, as he so cunningly had said. He showed to her a token, and gave her promise of good faith and friendly purpose. Then to her lord she said :

"Adam, my lord! This fruit is sweet and pleasing to the heart; this radiant messenger is God's good angel! I know by his attire he is a herald of our Lord, the King of heaven. Better to win his favour than his wrath! If thou to-day hast spoken aught of evil, yet will he still forgive thee, if we will do his will. Of what avail this bitter strife against the herald of thy Lord? We need his favour. For he may plead our cause before Almighty God, the King of heaven.

"I can behold where in the south and east He who shaped the world sits veiled in splendour. I see the angels circling round His throne, in winged flight, unnumbered myriads, clothed in beauty. Who could give me such discernment, except it be sent straight from God, the Lord of heaven? Widely may I hear and widely see through all the world across the broad creation. I hear the hymns of rapture from on high. Radiance blazes on my soul without and within since first I tasted of the fruit. Lo! my good lord! I bring thee in my hand this fruit, and give thee freely of it. I do believe that it is come from God, and brought by His command, as this messenger declared in words of truth. It is not like aught else on earth except, as this herald saith, it cometh straight from God."

Long she pled, and urged him all the day to that dark deed, to disobey their Lord's command. Close stood the evil fiend, inflaming with desire, luring with wiles, and boldly tempting him. The fiend stood near at hand who on that fatal mission had come a long, long way. He planned to hurl men down to utter death, mislead them and deceive them, that they might lose the gift of God, His favour and their heavenly realm. Lo! well the hell-fiend knew they must endure God's anger and the pains of hell, suffer grim misery and woe, since they had broken God's commandment, when with his lying words he tricked the beauteous maid, fairest of women, unto that deed of folly, so that she spake according to his will; and aided her in tempting unto evil [1] the handiwork of God.

Over and over the fairest of women pled with Adam, until she began to incline his heart so that he trusted the command the woman laid upon him. All this she did with good intent, and knew not that so many evils, such grim afflictions, would come upon mankind, when she was moved to hearken to the counsels of the evil herald; but she hoped to win God's favour by her words, showing such token and such pledge of truth unto the man, that the mind of Adam was changed within his breast, and his heart began to bend according to her will.

From the woman he took both death and hell, although it did not bear these names, but bore the name of fruit. The sleep of death and fiends' seduction; death and hell and exile and damnation — these were the fatal fruit whereon they feasted. And when the apple worked within him and touched his heart, then laughed aloud the evil-hearted fiend, capered about, and gave thanks to his lord for both:

[1] Grein: *on lalicne wroht*.

"Now have I won thy promised favour, and wrought thy will! For many a day to come is man undone, Adam and Eve! God's wrath shall be heavy upon them, for they have scorned His precepts and commandments. Wherefore they may no longer hold their heavenly kingdom, but they must travel the dark road to hell. Thou needest not feel sorrow in thy heart, as thou liest in thy bonds, nor mourn in spirit that men should dwell in heaven above, while we now suffer misery and pain in realms of darkness, and through thy pride have lost our high estate in heaven and goodly dwellings. God's anger was kindled against us because in heaven we would not bow our heads in service before the Holy Lord. It pleased us not to serve Him. Then was God moved to wrath and hard of heart, and drove us into hell; cast a great host into hell-fire, and with His hands prepared again in heaven celestial thrones, and gave that kingdom to mankind.

"Blithe be thy heart within thy breast! For here to-day are two things come to pass: the sons of men shall lose their heavenly kingdom, and journey unto thee to burn in flame; also heart-sorrow and affliction are visited on God. Whatever death we suffer here is now repaid on Adam in the wrath of God and man's damnation and the pangs of death. Therefore my heart is healed, my soul untrammelled in my breast. All our injuries are now avenged, and all the evil that we long have suffered. Now will I plunge again into the flame, and seek out Satan, where he lieth in hell's shadows, bound with chains."

Then the foul fiend sank downward to the wide-flung flames and gates of hell wherein his lord lay bound. But Adam and Eve were wretched in their hearts; sad were the words that passed between them. They feared the anger of the Lord their God; they dreaded the wrath of the King of heaven. They knew that His command was broken.

The woman mourned and wept in sorrow (she had forfeited God's grace and broken His commandment) when she beheld the radiance disappear which he who brought this evil on them had showed her by a faithless token, that they might suffer pangs of hell and untold woe. Wherefore heart-sorrow burned within their breasts. Husband and wife they bowed them down in prayer, beseeching God and calling on the Lord of heaven, and prayed that they might expiate their sin, since they had broken God's commandment. They saw that their bodies were naked. In that land they had as yet no settled home, nor knew they aught of pain or sorrow; but they might have prospered in the land if they had done God's will. Many a rueful word they uttered, husband and wife together. And Adam spake unto Eve and said:

"O Eve! a bitter portion hast thou won us! Dost thou behold the yawning gulf of hell, sunless, insatiate? Thou mayest hear the groans that rise therefrom! The heavenly realm is little like that blaze of fire! Lo! fairest of all lands is this, which we, by God's grace, might have held hadst thou not hearkened unto him who urged this evil, so that we set at naught the word of God, the King of heaven. Now in grief we mourn that evil mission! For God Himself bade us beware of sin and dire disaster. Now thirst and hunger press upon my heart whereof we formerly were ever free. How shall we live or dwell now in this land if the wind blow from the west or east, south or north, if mist arise and showers of hail beat on us from the heavens, and frost cometh, wondrous cold, upon the earth, or, hot in heaven, shineth the burning sun, and we two stand here naked and unclothed? We have no shelter from the weather, nor any store of food. And the Mighty Lord, our God, is angry with us. What shall become of us? Now I repent me that I prayed the God of heaven, the Gracious Lord, and of my limbs He wrought thee for my helpmeet, since thou hast led me unto evil and the anger of my Lord. Well may

I repent to all eternity that ever I beheld thee with mine eyes!"

Then spake Eve, the lovely maid, fairest of women. (She was the work of God, though led astray by power of the fiend):

"Well mayest thou upbraid me, my dear Adam! But thou canst not repent one whit more bitterly in thy heart than my heart repenteth."

And Adam answered her: "If I but knew the will of God, the penalty I needs must pay, thou couldest not find one more swift to do it, though the Lord of heaven bade me go forth and walk upon the sea. The ocean-stream could never be so wondrous deep or wide that ever my heart would doubt, but I would go even unto the bottom of the sea, if I might work the will of God. I have no wish for years of manhood in the world now that I have forfeited the favour of my Lord, and lost His grace. But we may not be thus together, naked. Let us go into this grove, and under the shelter of this wood."

And they turned and went weeping into the green wood, and sat them down apart from one another to wait the fate the Lord of heaven should assign them, since they had lost their former state and portion which Almighty God had given them. And they covered their bodies with leaves, and clothed them with the foliage of the wood, for they had no garments. And both together bowed in prayer; and every morning they besought Almighty God, the Gracious Lord, that He would not forget them, but would teach them how to live thenceforward in the light.

(End of Genesis B)

Then came Almighty God, the Glorious Prince, walking in the garden after the midday, according to His will. Our Saviour, the Merciful Father, would fain discover what His children did. He knew their glory was gone which formerly He gave them. Sadly they stole away into the darkness of the trees, bereft of glory, and hid themselves in the shadows when they heard the holy voice of God, and were afraid. Then the Lord of heaven began to call the warden of the world, and bade His son come quickly unto Him. And he made answer unto God, and spake of his nakedness with shame:

"I will clothe my nakedness with a garment, my dear Lord, and cover my shame with leaves. My heart is troubled and cast down within me. I dare not come before Thy presence, for I am naked."

And straightway God made answer unto him: "Tell me, My son, why stealest thou away into the darkness with shame? Thou didst not formerly feel shame before Me, but only joy. Wherefore art thou humbled and abashed, knowing sorrow, covering thy body with leaves, sad of heart and wretched in thy woe, saying thou needest clothing, except thou hast eaten of the fruit of the tree which I forbade thee?"

And Adam again made answer: "My Lord! this woman, this lovely maid, gave me the fruit into my hand, and I took it in trespass against Thee. And now I clearly bear the token upon me and know the more of sorrow."

Then Almighty God questioned Eve: "Of what avail, My daughter, were My abundant blessings, the new-created Paradise and pleasant growing things, that thou shouldest stretch thy hands with yearning unto the tree, and pluck the apples growing on its boughs, and eat the deadly fruit in trespass against Me, and give to Adam, when by My word it was forbidden to you both?"

And the lovely woman, put to shame, made answer: "The serpent, the deadly snake, with fair words tempted me, and eagerly enticed me to that deed of sin and evil appetite, until I basely did the deed and wrought the wrong, despoiled the tree within the wood, as was not right, and ate the fruit."

Then our Saviour, the Almighty Lord, decreed unto the serpent, the guilty snake, an endless wandering, and said:

"All thy life upon thy belly shalt thou go to and fro upon the fields of the broad earth,

accursed, so long as life and spirit dwell within
thee. Dust shalt thou eat all the days of thy
life for the grievous evil thou hast wrought.
The woman shall loathe and hate thee under
heaven. Her foot shall crush thy head, and
thou shalt bruise her heel anew. There shall
be strife between your seed for ever, while
the world standeth under heaven. Now
thou knowest clearly, thou foul tempter, what
thy life shall be."

And unto Eve God spake in wrath : " Turn
thee from joy ! Thou shalt live under man's
dominion, sore smitten with fear before him.
With bitter sorrow shalt thou expiate thy
sin, waiting for death, bringing forth sons
and daughters in the world with grief and
tears and lamentation."

And on Adam the Eternal God, Author of
life, pronounced an evil doom : " Thou shalt
seek another home, a joyless dwelling. Naked
and needy shalt thou suffer exile, shorn of
thy glory. Thy soul and body shall be cleft
asunder. Lo ! thou hast sinned a grievous
sin. Therefore shalt thou labour, winning
thy portion on the earth by toil, eating thy
bread in the sweat of thy brow while thou
dwellest here, until that grim disease, which
first thou tasted in the apple, shall grip hard
at thy heart. So shalt thou die."

Lo ! now we know how our afflictions came
upon us, and mortal misery ! Then the Lord
of glory, our Creator, clothed them with gar-

ments, and bade them cover their shame with their first raiment. He drove them forth from Paradise into a narrower life. By God's command a holy angel, with a sword of fire, closed fast that pleasant home of peace and joy behind them. No wicked, sinful man may walk therein, but the warden has strength and power, dear unto God in virtue, who guards that life of glory.

Yet the Almighty Father would not take away from Adam and from Eve, at once, all goodly things, though He withdrew His favour from them. But for their comfort He left the sky above them adorned with shining stars, gave them wide-stretching fields, and bade the earth and sea and all their teeming multitudes to bring forth fruits to serve man's earthly need. After their sin they dwelt in a realm more sorrowful, a home and native land less rich in all good things than was their first abode, wherefrom He drove them out after their sin.

Then, according to the word of God, Adam and Eve begat children, as God had bidden. To them were born two goodly sons, Abel and Cain: the books tell us how these brothers, first of toilers, gained wealth and goods and store of food. One, the first-born, tilled the fields; the other aided with his father's cattle; and after many days they both brought offerings to God. The Prince of angels, Lord of every creature, lifted up His eyes on Abel's offering and would not look upon the gift of Cain. And the heart of Cain was bitter; wrath shook his soul, and envy burned within him. Then with his hands Cain wrought a deed of shame, struck down his brother Abel, and poured his blood upon the ground. The earth drank in his blood poured out in murder.

After that mortal blow came woe and tribulation. From that shoot grew more and more a deadly bitter fruit, and the boughs of sin stretched far and wide among the nations; grievously the twigs of evil touched the sons of men (and do so yet), and from them grew broad blades of wickedness. With lamentation must we tell that tale of evil fate, not without cause. Grievous the ruin the lovely woman wrought us by that first of sins that ever men on earth had sinned against their Maker since Adam first was filled with breath from the mouth of God.

Then the Lord of glory spake unto Cain, and asked where Abel was. Quickly the cursed fashioner of death made answer unto Him:

"I know not the coming or going of Abel, my kinsman, his lot or portion; I was not my brother's keeper."

And the Gracious Spirit, Lord of angels, made answer unto him: "Why hast thou slain that faithful man thy brother in thy wrath, and his blood calleth and crieth unto

Me? Accursed for ever, driven into exile, thou shalt be punished for this deed of death! The earth shall not yield thee of her pleasant fruits for thy daily need, but by thy hands her soil is stained with holy blood. Therefore the green earth shall withhold from thee her beauty and her delights. In sadness and dishonour shalt thou depart from thy home, because thou hast slain thy brother, Abel. Loathed of thy kinsmen, an exile and a fugitive, shalt thou wander on the face of the earth."

And Cain made answer unto Him: . . . "I need not look for pity in this world, High King of heaven, for I have lost Thy love and favour and goodwill. Weary the ways my feet must wander, in dread of woe, whenever one shall meet me in my guilt, near or far, and by his hate remind me of my brother's death. I shed his blood and poured his life-blood on the ground. From this day hast Thou cut me off from good! Thou scourgest me from home! Some cruel foe shall slay me. And I must needs go forth, accursed, from Thy sight, O Lord!"

And the Lord of victory said unto him: "Thou needest not yet dread death, nor the pangs of death, though thou shalt wander, far from kinsmen, with thy doom upon thee. If any man shall slay thee with his hands, on him shall fall a seven-fold vengeance, and torment for that deed of sin."

And God, the Lord of glory, set a mark upon him and a token, lest any foe from far or near should dare to lift his hand against him; and He bade him go forth in his guilt from mother and kinsmen and from all his tribe. Then with despairing heart, a friendless exile, Cain departed out of the sight of God, and chose a home and dwelling in the eastern lands, far from his father's house; and there a comely maiden bare him children after his kind.

Enoch was first-born of the sons of Cain. He built a city with his kinsmen, the first of all those strongholds under heaven which sword-girt men established; and in the city sons were born to him. Irad was first-born of the sons of Enoch; and he begat children, and all the tribe and race of Cain increased. And after Irad Mahalaleel was warden of the treasure, in his father's stead, until he died. Then Methusael dispensed the treasure to his brothers and his kinsmen, man for man, till, full of many years, he died.

And at his father's death Lamech succeeded to the treasure and the household goods. Two wives bare children to him in his home, Adah and Zillah. Now one of the sons of Lamech was called Jabal; and he was first of all men by his skill to stir the harp to music and its strings to song. And there was also in that tribe another son of Lamech, called Tubal Cain, a smith skilled in his craft. He was the first of all men on the earth to fashion tools of husbandry; and far and wide the city-dwelling sons of men made use of bronze and iron.

Then to his two beloved wives, Adah and Zillah, Lamech rehearsed a tale of shame: "I have struck down a kinsman unto death! I have defiled my hands with the blood of Cain! I smote down Enoch's father, slayer of Abel, and poured his blood upon the ground. Full well I know that for that mortal deed shall come God's seven-fold vengeance. With fearful torment shall my deed of death and murder be requited, when I go hence."

Then another son was born to Adam in Abel's stead; and his name was Seth. He was a righteous son and blessed, a solace to his parents, his father and mother, Adam and Eve. And he filled the place of Abel in the world. Then Adam spake, the first of men:

"The eternal God of victory, the Lord of life, hath vouchsafed me another son in place of my beloved whom Cain slew. So our Lord hath stilled the sorrow of my heart. To Him be thanks!"

Now, when Adam begat another son to be his heir, that sturdy man had lived an hundred and thirty winters of this life in the world. The writings tell us that Adam increased his tribe on earth, begetting sons and daughters eight hundred years. And all the years of Adam were nine hundred and thirty winters, and he died.

And Seth succeeded Adam: at his father's death the well-loved son possessed the treasure, and took himself a wife. And Seth lived an hundred and five winters in the world and increased his tribe, begetting sons and daughters. Enos was first-born of the sons of Seth; and he was first of all the sons of men to call upon the name of God since Adam, first a living spirit, set foot on the green earth. Seth prospered, eight hundred and seven winters begetting sons and daughters. And all the years of Seth were nine hundred and twelve winters, and he died.

And after he went hence, and the earth received the body of seed-bearing Seth, Enos was warden of the heritage. Dear was he unto God! He lived for ninety winters in the world, and begat children. And Cainan was first-born of the sons of Enos. Eight hundred and fifteen winters the man of wisdom lived, at peace with God, begetting sons and daughters. And all the years of Enos were nine hundred and five winters, and he died.

And after Enos Cainan ruled the tribe as lord and leader. He lived seventy winters, and begat a son. An heir was born unto his house, and his name was Mahalaleel.

Eight hundred and forty winters Cainan lived, and increased his tribe. And all the years of the son of Enos were nine hundred and ten winters, and he died, and his appointed days beneath the heavens were fulfilled.

And after Cainan Mahalaleel possessed the land and treasure many a year. The prince lived five-and-sixty winters, and begat a son. An heir was born unto his house, and his kinsmen called him Jared, as I have heard. Mahalaleel lived long, enjoying bliss on earth, the joys of men, and worldly treasure. And all the years of Mahalaleel were eight hundred five-and-ninety winters, and he died, and gave the land and rule unto his son.

A long time Jared dealt out gold to men. He was a righteous prince, a noble earl, dear to his kinsmen. He lived an hundred five-and-sixty winters in the world, and, when her time was come, his wife brought forth her first-born, a goodly son. And his name was Enoch. Eight hundred years his father lived, and increased his tribe. And all the years of Jared were nine hundred five-and-sixty winters, and he died, and gave the land and rule unto his son, the wise and well-loved prince.

And Enoch ruled the folk, led them in ways of peace, and no wise let his sway and power lessen, while he was lord over his kinsmen. Now Enoch prospered and in-

creased his tribe three hundred years. And
God, the Lord of heaven, was gracious unto
him! In his natural body he entered into
heavenly joy and the glory of God, dying
no mortal death as men do here, the young
and old, what time God taketh from them
wealth and substance and earthly treasure
and their life; but with the King of angels
he departed still alive out of this fleeting life,
in the same vestments which his soul received
before his mother bare him. He left the
people to his eldest son. And all the years
of Enoch were three hundred five-and-sixty
winters, and he died.

Then Methuselah held sway among his
kinsmen, and longest of all men enjoyed the
pleasures of this world. He begat a multitude
of sons and daughters before his death. And
all the years of Methuselah were nine hundred
and seventy winters, and he died.

And Lamech, his son, succeeded him and
kept the treasure. Long time he ruled the
land. He lived an hundred and two winters,
and begat children. And the lord and
leader of the folk lived five hundred five-and-
ninety years, enjoying many winters under
heaven, ruling the folk with wisdom. And
Lamech increased his tribe, begetting sons
and daughters. He called the name of the
first-born Noah; and Noah ruled the land
after the death of Lamech.

Now Noah, the lord of men, lived five

hundred winters, as the books say, and begat children. The first-born son of Noah was Shem, and the second Ham, and the third Japheth. And the folk grew in number under heaven, and the multitude of the race of men increased throughout the earth. The tribe of Seth, the well-loved prince, was still exceeding dear to God, and blessed in His love!

Then the sons of God began to take them wives from the tribe of Cain, a cursed folk, and the sons of men chose them wives from among that people, the fair and winsome daughters of that sinful race, against the will of God. Then the Lord of heaven lifted up His voice in wrath against mankind, and said:

"Lo! I have not been unmindful of the sons of men, but the tribe of Cain hath sorely angered Me. The sons of Seth have stirred My wrath against them; they have taken them wives from among the daughters of My foes. Woman's beauty and woman's grace and the eternal fiend have taken hold upon this people who dwelt of old in peace."

An hundred and twenty numbered winters in the world that fated folk were busied in evil. Then the Lord resolved to punish those faithless spirits, and slay the sinful giant sons, undear to God, those huge, unholy scathers, loathsome to the Lord. The King of victory beheld how great was the wickedness of men on earth, and saw that they were bold in sin and full of wiles. He resolved to bring destruction on the tribes of men, and smite mankind with heavy hand. It repented Him exceedingly that He had made man, and the first of men, when He created Adam. He said that for the sins of men He would lay waste the earth, and all that was upon the earth, destroying every living thing that breathed the breath of life. All this would the Lord destroy in the days that were coming on the sons of men.

But Noah, the son of Lamech, was good and dear to God, exceeding blessed, just and meek. And the Lord knew that virtue flourished in the heart of Noah. Wherefore God, the Holy Lord of every creature, spake unto Noah, declaring His wrath and vengeance on the sons of men. For He saw that the earth was full of wickedness, and its broad and fertile meadows filled with sin and defiled with uncleanness. And the Lord our God spake unto Noah, and said :

"I will destroy this people with a flood, man and every living thing that the air and the seas bring forth and nourish, birds of the air and beasts of the field. But thou, and thy sons with thee, shall have mercy when the black waters, the dark, destroying floods, shall overwhelm the hosts of sinful men. Begin to build thee a ship, a mighty sea-house, and in it make abiding-room for many, and set a rightful place for every tribe of earth. Build floors within the ark, dividing it in stories. And thou shalt build it three hundred cubits long and fifty cubits wide and thirty cubits high, and fasten it firmly against the might of the waves. And thou shalt take within the ark the seed of every living thing, and the offspring of all flesh upon the earth. And the ark must hold them all."

And Noah did according as God commanded him. He hearkened unto the Holy King of heaven, and began straightway to build the ark, a mighty sea-chest. And unto his kinsmen he proclaimed destruction coming upon men, and bitter vengeance. And they heeded him not.

Then after many winters the Faithful Lord beheld the greatest of ocean-houses, Noah's vessel, towering up, made tight with the best of pitch within and without against the floods. And it was best of all its kind, growing more hard the more the rough waves and the black sea-streams beat up against it. Then our Lord said unto Noah:

"I give thee My pledge, dearest of men, that thou mayest go thy way, thou and the seed of every living thing which thou shalt ferry through the deep water for many a day in the bosom of the ship. Lead on board the ark, as I bid thee, thy household, thy wife and thy three sons, and thy sons' wives with thee. And take within that sea-home seven of every kind of living thing that serve as food for men, and two of every other kind. Likewise of all the fruits of the earth take food for the company upon thy ship, who with thee shall be saved from the flood! Care well for every creature until I shall cause food to grow again beneath the heavens for the survivors of the ocean floods. Depart now with thy household and thy host of guests, embarking on the ship. I know that thou art good, and of a steadfast mind. Thou art worthy of grace and mercy, thou and thy children. Lo! for seven nights I shall let the rains descend upon the face of the broad earth. Forty days will I visit My wrath upon men, with a deluge destroying the riches of the world and the tribes of men, save what shall be upon the ark when the black floods begin to rise."

And Noah departed, as the Lord commanded, embarking his household upon the ark, leading up his sons into the ship, and their wives with them. All that Almighty God would have for seed went in under the roof of the ark unto their food-giver, even according as the Mighty Lord of hosts gave bidding by His word. And the Warden of that heavenly kingdom, the God of victories, locked the door of the ocean-house behind him with His hands, and our Lord blessed all within the ark with His blessing. Now Noah, the son of Lamech, had lived six hundred winters, wise and full of years, when he went up with the young men, his beloved sons, into the ark, as God gave bidding.

Then the Lord sent the rains from heaven, and caused the black sea-streams to roar, and the fountains of the deep to overflow the world. The seas surged up over the barriers of the shore. Mighty in His wrath was He who rules the waters! And He overwhelmed and covered the mortal sons of sin with a black deluge, laying waste the native land and homes of men. God visited their offences upon them. Forty days and forty nights the sea laid hold on that doomed folk. Dire was that disaster and deadly unto men. The stormy surges of the King of glory quenched the life from out the bodies of that sinful host. The flood, raging beneath the heavens, covered over all high hills throughout the spacious earth, and lifted up the ark from the earth upon the bosom of the waters, and all within the ark, whom the Lord our God had blessed when He locked the door of the ship. Then far and wide that best of ocean-houses and its burden floated beneath the heavens over the compass of the sea. The raging terrors of the deep might not lay hold on ship or mariners, but Holy God ferried them upon the sea and shielded them. Fifteen cubits deep upon the hills the deluge lay. That was a grievous fate!

But no harm came nigh unto the ark, save that it was lifted up to heaven, when the flood destroyed all creatures on the earth; but Holy God, the Eternal King, the Lord of heaven, stern of heart, preserved the ark when He unleashed the ocean currents and their changing streams. And God, the Lord of victory, was mindful of those mariners, of the son of Lamech, and all the living things which the Author of life and light had locked within the bosom of the ship against the waters' might. The Lord of hosts guided the warriors by His word across the world.

Then the welling floods began to lessen and the black tides ebbed beneath the heavens. The Just God turned the waters again from His children, and stilled the downpour of the rains. Foamy-necked the ship fared on an hundred and fifty nights beneath the heavens, after the flood had lifted up that best of vessels with its well-nailed sides—until at last the appointed number of the days of wrath were passed away.

And the ark of Noah, the greatest of seahomes, with its burden, rested high upon the hills which are called Armenia. There the holy son of Lamech waited many days for God's faithful covenant to be fulfilled, when the Warden of life, the Lord Almighty, would give him respite from the perils he had suffered while the black waves bore him far and wide upon the waters over the spacious earth.

The floods receded, and those sea-tossed men, together with their wives, longed for the hour when they might leave their narrow home, and step across the well-nailed sides upon the shore, and from their prison lead out their possessions. And Noah, the helmsman of the ark, made trial whether the sea-floods yet were ebbing under heaven. After many days, while the high hills yet harboured the seed and treasure of the tribes of earth, the son of Lamech let a dusky raven fly forth from the ark over the deep flood. And Noah was sure that in its need, if so be it should find no land upon this journey, the raven would return to him again within the ark across the wide water. But Noah's hope failed him! Exulting the raven perched upon the floating bodies of the dead; the black-winged bird would not return.

And seven days after the dusky raven he let a grey dove fly forth from the ark across the deep water, making trial whether the high and foaming floods had yet receded from any region of the green earth. Widely she sought her heart's desire, circling afar, but nowhere finding rest. Because of the floods she might not set foot upon the land, nor settle on the branch of any tree because of the ocean-streams. The high hills were covered by the deep. And so at evening over the dusky wave the wild bird sought the ark, settling hungry and weary into the hands of that holy man.

And again after seven days a second dove was sent forth from the ark. The wild bird circled widely till she found a refuge and a pleasant resting-place, and settled in a tree. Blithe of heart, she rejoiced that in her weariness she might find rest upon its pleasant branches. She shook her feathers and flew back with a gift, bearing as she flew a branch of an olive tree with its green blades. And the prince of shipmen knew that comfort was at hand, and a requital of their toilsome voyage.

And again after seven days the blessed man sent forth a third wild dove. And she flew not back unto the ark, but came to land and the green forests. Her heart was glad; never again would she appear under the black roof of the ark. Nor was there need! Then our Lord, the Warden of the heavenly kingdom, with holy word spake unto Noah:

" For thee again on earth a fair abiding-place is founded, blessings upon the land, and rest from far sea-wandering. Depart in peace out of the ark; go forth upon the bosom of the earth. And from the high ship lead thy household, and all the living things which graciously I shielded against the flood, so long as the sea held sway and covered thy third home."

1460–1492

And Noah hearkened unto God with great rejoicing, and did according as the Voice commanded. And he went out upon the shore, and led forth from the ark all who had survived that time of woe. Then Noah, wise of counsel, began to offer sacrifice to God. And for an offering he took a part of all his goods which God had given him to enjoy, and, great in wisdom and in glory, made sacrifice to God, the King of angels. And straightway our Lord made known that He had blessed Noah, and Noah's children, because he had offered that thank-offering, and in his youth by good deeds had deserved the bounteous mercies which Almighty God in majesty bestowed upon him. And God, the Lord of glory, spake unto Noah and said :

"Be fruitful and multiply, enjoying honour, delighting in peace. Fill all the earth with your increase. To you is given the home of your fathers, dominion over the fish of the sea, and the fowls of the air, and the beasts of the field, over all the green earth and its teeming herds. Never shall ye eat in blood your shameful feasts through sin defiled with blood. For most he injureth himself and his soul's honour whoso shall slay another with the sword. Verily ! in no wise shall his heart have joy in his reward ! For many times more heavily will I avenge man's life upon his murderer, because his sword hath prospered in violence and blood, and his hands in death. Man was first fashioned in the image of God. Each hath the form of God and of the angels, whoso will keep My holy laws.

"Be fruitful and multiply, enjoying grace on earth and every pleasant thing. Fill all the regions of the earth with your increase, your issue, and your seed. And unto you I give My covenant that never again will I bring the waters upon the earth or a flood on the wide-stretching land. Oft shall ye behold the token of My promise in the heavens, when I show forth My rainbow, that I will keep this covenant with men while the world standeth."

And the wise son of Lamech, the warden of wealth, came forth from the ship as the flood receded, and his three sons with him. And their four wives were called Percoba, and Olla, and Olliva, and Ollivani. The Faithful Lord had saved them to survive the flood.[1] And Noah's stout-hearted sons were Shem and Ham, and the third was Japheth. From them sprang many peoples, and all the earth was filled with the sons of men.

Then a second time Noah began to establish a home with his kinsmen, and to till the earth for food. He toiled and wrought and planted a vineyard and sowed seed, and laboured that the green earth might bring

---

[1] Grein: *þa wið flode nerede frea ælmihtig.*

forth her shining harvests, her gleaming crops, in every season.

And it came to pass upon a time that the blessed man lay drunk with wine in his dwelling, and slumbered heavy with feasting, and cast off his robe from his body, as was not seemly, and lay there naked of limb. Little did he know what evil plight was his in his dwelling, while drunkenness had hold upon his heart within him in its holy house. But his soul was fast bound in slumber, so that in his stupor he might not cover himself with a garment, nor hide his shame, as was decreed for man and woman what time the thane of glory with a sword of fire behind our first great parents locked the gates of life.

Then Ham, the son of Noah, went in where his lord lay sleeping, and would not look with reverence upon his father, nor cover his shame. But he laughed, and told his brothers how their lord lay sleeping in his home. And straightway, covering their faces with their cloaks, they went in unto the well-beloved to bring him succour. For both were good of heart, both Shem and Japheth.

Then the son of Lamech awoke from his slumber, and learned that Ham had failed to show him reverence or love when he had greatest need. And the holy man was grieved in his heart, and set a curse upon his son, saying that Ham should be an outcast under heaven and servant to his kinsmen on the earth. And the curse lay heavy upon him and on all his tribe. And Noah and his sons as freemen ruled a wide-stretching realm for three hundred and fifty winters of this life, after the flood. Then he went hence. And his sons possessed his wealth, and begat children and prospered.

Children were born unto Japheth, a glad hearth-band of sons and daughters. He was a godly man, enjoying bliss and blessing with his children, until his soul within his breast, ready to depart, must needs go forth unto the glory of God. And Gormer, Japheth's son, dispensed his father's treasure among his friends and kinsmen, near and dear. And no little portion of the earth was filled with their increase.

Likewise sons were born unto Ham. The names of the eldest were called Cush and Ham, two goodly youths, his first-born sons. And Cush was ruler of his tribe, dispensing joy and worldly wealth and treasure unto his brothers in his father's stead, after Ham died, and his soul departed from this earthly body. He ruled his tribe and gave them laws until his days were run. Then he gave over earthly riches and sought another life and his Father's bosom.[1]

And the first-born son of Cush, a far-famed man, held his ancestral seat. The writings

---

[1] Grein: *hreðer* for *breðer*.

tell us that of all men then alive his strength and power were greatest. He was lord of the kingdom of Babylon, and first of princes to exalt her glory. He enlarged her borders and brought her fame. Now there was yet one common tongue for all men on the earth. And a great tribe was born of the stem of Ham and a mighty people spreading far and wide.

And Shem begat a host of free-born sons and daughters, and, after many winters, went to his last rest. In that tribe men were good! One of the sons of Shem was Eber, and from him sprang a countless race which all men dwelling in the earth call Hebrews. They departed out of the east, taking with them all their substance, their cattle and their goods. That was a dauntless folk! The heroes sought a roomier land, a wandering folk, in mighty multitudes, and chose at last a fixed abode wherein to settle. Far and wide in days of old the leaders of that people, with their well-loved men, possessed the land of Shinar, a land of green plains and pleasant valleys. And at that time they prospered greatly, and had abundance of all good things.

Then many a man besought his friend, and one stout warrior urged another, that, before their multitude and the tribes of their people should be scattered again over the face of the whole earth in search of land, they should build a city to their glory and rear a tower

1630–1667

unto the stars of heaven, to be a sign that they had sought the land of Shinar, where of old the mighty leaders of the folk had lived at ease. And they sought out men for this work and deed of sin, in rash pride showing forth their strength. Greedy for glory, they reared a city with their hands, and raised a ladder up to heaven, and in their vain strength built a wall of stone beyond the measure of men.

Then came Holy God to look upon the work of the children of men, the citadel and the tower which the sons of Adam were beginning to rear unto heaven. Stern of heart, the King reproved their folly, and in His wrath confounded the tongues of the dwellers of earth, and they might not prosper in their speech. Then the leaders of the work in pride of strength met together about the tower in many bands. But no one band could understand another. And they left off to build the wall of stone, and were wretchedly sundered into tribes divided by their speech. And every tribe became alien to every other tribe, when the Lord in His might sundered the speech of men. So the divided sons of men were scattered on four ways in search of land. And behind them the steadfast tower of stone, and the high citadel, stood unfinished together in the land of Shinar.

Now the tribe of Shem increased and
1667–1703

flourished under heaven. And a certain man of that tribe, of thoughtful heart and given to virtue, had noble children. Two goodly sons were born to him, and bred in Babylon, great-hearted princes named Abraham and Haran. And the Lord of angels was their guide and friend. Now Haran had a noble son, whose name was Lot. And Abraham and Lot throve excellently before the Lord as was their nature from their elders. Wherefore men proclaim their virtues far and wide upon the earth.

Then was the time fulfilled, and Abraham brought a wife unto his home, a fair and comely woman to his dwelling. And her name was Sarah, as the writings tell us. Many a winter they enjoyed the world, prospering in peace for many a year. But it was not given unto Abraham that his comely wife should bear him children, or an heir unto his house.

And Abraham's father went out with his household, and with all their substance, journeying through the realm of the Chaldeans. Fain would the wise lord with his kinsfolk seek the land of Canaan. And Abraham and Lot, his kinsmen, dear to God, departed with him out of that country. The noble sons of men chose them a dwelling in the land of Haran, and their wives with them. And Abraham's father, the faithful, died in that land. And all his years were two hundred and five winters, and he departed, full of years, to see God.

Then the Holy Warden of the heavenly kingdom, Eternal God, said unto Abraham: "Go forth from this place, and lead thy household and thy cattle with thee. Get thee out of the land of Haran, and from thy father's home. Journey as I bid thee, dearest of men; hearken to My teachings, and seek the land of green, wide-stretching plains, which I shall show thee. Blessed shalt thou live in My protection. If any of the dwellers of earth greet thee with evil, him will I curse for thy sake; and I will set My anger upon him and My enduring wrath. But unto them that honour thee will I be gracious and give them all their heart's desire. Through thee all nations dwelling in the earth shall have My peace and friendship, My bliss and blessing in the world. The number of thy tribe, thy sons and daughters, shall be increased beneath the heavens, until the earth and many a land shall be filled with thy seed."

And Abraham, great in virtue and blessed with gold and silver, departed with much substance out of the land of Haran, leading his herds and his possessions, even unto the borders of the Egyptians, according as our God, the Lord of victory, commanded by His word, and sought a dwelling in the land of Canaan. Beloved of God, he came with gladness to that land, and his wife with him, the dear companion of his bed, and the wife of his brother's son. And his years were five-and-seventy winters when he went out from the land of Haran, and from his kinsmen. And Abraham was mindful of the words of the Almighty Father, and journeyed through all the borders of that people, at his Lord's behest, to view the land afar, and came at last in safety, with undaunted heart, to Sichem and the Canaanites. And the Just Lord, the King of angels, revealed Himself to Abraham and said :

"This is the roomy land, the beautiful, green realm, adorned with increase, which I will give thy seed to rule."

And there the prince builded an altar to the Lord, and offered up a sacrifice to God, the Lord of life, Protector of all souls. And Abraham departed again out of the east to view with his eyes this best of lands (and he was mindful of the gracious promise which the Heavenly Warden, the Lord of victory, had given by His holy word) until they came with their multitudes unto a village called Bethel. Out of the east their leader, blithe of heart, and his brother's son, God-fearing men, journeyed with all their substance through far-famed lands, and over high, steep hills, and chose a dwelling where the fields seemed wondrous fair. And again Abraham builded an altar, calling earnestly on God, and offered sacrifice unto the Lord of life. And God was gracious, and with unsparing hand granted him reward upon the altar.

And for a time thereafter the prince abode in his dwellings, and his wife with him, enjoying all good things, until a grievous famine fell upon the tribes of Canaan, and bitter hunger, grim as death to men within their homes. Then Abraham, wise of heart, and chosen of the Lord, betook him into Egypt to seek a place of refuge. The faithful hero fled from that affliction; too bitter was the woe. And, in the wisdom of his heart, when he beheld the gabled palaces and high-walled towns of the Egyptians gleaming brightly, Abraham began to speak unto his wife and counsel her:

"Lo! many a proud Egyptian shall behold thy beauty, maiden of elfin grace! And if one look upon thee with desire, thinking thou art my wife, I fear lest, in his longing for thy love, some foe may slay me with the sword. Therefore, Sarah, say thou art my sister and my kin, if any stranger question what the bond may be between us two of alien race and distant home. Conceal the truth! So shalt thou save my life if God, our Lord Almighty, who sent us on this journey, that we might strive for honour and advantage among the Egyptians, will grant me His protection as of old, and longer life."

So Abraham, the dauntless earl, came

journeying with all his substance into Egypt, where men were alien to him and friends unknown. And many a proud earl, great in glory, found the woman fair; to many a bold thane of the king she seemed of royal beauty; and this they told their lord. They little thought of any fairer maid, but praised the winsome loveliness of Sarah more highly to their prince, until he bade them bring the lovely woman to his hall. And the lord of men, dispenser of treasure, bade them show honour upon Abraham. But the Lord God visited His anger upon Pharaoh because of his love of the woman; bitterly the prince of men atoned, and all his household. He knew why the Lord afflicted him with plagues! Then the prince of Egypt called Abraham before him, who was sore afraid; and he gave him his wife again and his consort, and bade him seek friends elsewhere, other princes and another folk. And he bade his thanes and serving men conduct him, uninjured and with honour, out from among that people, that he might be at peace.

So Abraham took his possessions and went out from the land of Egypt. Brave men conveyed the maiden, the bride with rings adorned, and they led their flocks and earthly riches unto Bethel to their olden dwellings again, wife and wealth and worldly treasure. They began to build there, to found a city, and renew their halls and establish a home.

1844-1881

And they builded an altar in the plain near that which Abraham had built aforetime to his God, when he came out of the west. And there the blessed man of noble heart gave praise anew unto the name of the Eternal Lord, offering sacrifice unto the Prince of angels, and giving thanks abundantly unto the Lord of life for all His grace and mercy.

Then Abraham and Lot abode in that place, having the fullness of their desires, enjoying bliss, until no longer could they prosper in that land together, with their possessions, but those righteous men must needs seek elsewhere some roomier dwelling-place. For often quarrels rose between the followers of these faithful men, and strife among their shepherds. Then holy Abraham, mindful of honour, spake fairly unto Lot:

"I am thy father's brother in blood kinship, and thou my brother's son. No strife shall rise, no feud grow up, between us two. God will not suffer that. We two are kinsmen; naught else shall there be between us save goodness and enduring love. Now, Lot, take thought how strong men dwell about our borders, mighty tribes with thanes and allies, men of valour, the tribe of the Canaanites and the tribe of the Perizzites. They will not give us of their land! Therefore let us go forth from this place, and seek out roomier fields. I give good counsel, son of Haran, for us both, and speak the truth. I give thee choice, my son! Take thought, and ponder in thy heart on which hand thou wilt bend thy course, thou and thy cattle. The choice is thine!"

Then Lot departed to view the green earth and the land that lies by Jordan. And it was watered with rivers, and covered with pleasant fruits, bright with running streams, and like the Paradise of God before our Lord gave over Sodom and Gomorrah unto fire and black flame, because of the sins of men. And there the son of Haran chose him a dwelling and a settlement in the city of Sodom. . . . And thither he took[1] from Bethel all his substance, rings and household treasure and riches and twisted gold. And he abode by Jordan many a year. The place was fair, but those that dwelt therein were impious and hateful unto God. The race of Sodomites were bold in sin, in deeds perverse, working eternal folly. Lot would not adopt the customs of that people, but turned him from their practices, their sin and shame, though he must needs dwell in the land. He kept him pure and spotless and of patient heart among that people, mindful of God's commands, most like as if he knew not what that nation did.

And Abraham abode thenceforth in the

[1] Grein: *lædde eall þider*.

dwellings of the Canaanites. And the Lord of men, the King of angels, was his defender, granting him his heart's desires and worldly wealth and love and favour. Wherefore the tribes of men, the children of baptism, exalt his praise full widely under heaven. He served the Lord with gladness while he lived on earth, holy and wise of heart. Never need any man lack shelter or defence, nor be afraid and fearful before God, whoso, in return for His protection,[1] with discerning heart, with wit and word and understanding, in thought and deed will serve Him till his death!

Then, as I have heard, Chedorlaomer, king of the Elamites, a bold folk-captain, marshalled an army, and Amraphel of Shinar and a mighty host [2] were joined with him. Four kings with a great multitude departed into the south against Sodom and Gomorrah. And all the land about Jordan was overrun with armed men and hostile bands. Many a trembling maiden, pale with fear, must needs endure a foe's embrace. Many a warrior perished, sick with wounds, guarding their wives and treasure.

Against them from the south five kings went forth to war with battle-hosts and marching squadrons. Fain would they

---

[1] Grein: *mundbyrde*.
[2] *Ibid.*: *worude* for *worulde*.

guard the city of Sodom against the foe. Twelve winters long that folk had given toll and tribute to the Northmen, and would no more enrich the lord of Elam with their treasure, but they rebelled against him. Onward the hosts advanced, intent on death. (Loud sang the javelins.) Amid the spears the blackbird, dewy-feathered, croaked in hope of carrion. In multitudes, with steadfast hearts, the warriors hastened till the hosts were gathered from afar, from south and north, helmeted men.

Then was hard hand-play; crashing of weapons, storming of death-darts, tumult of battle. From out the sheaths men snatched their ring-decked, keen-edged swords. There might an earl have his fill of fighting, whoso was not yet sated with war. The Northmen smote the people of the south. In the shock of shields the men of Sodom and Gomorrah, dispensers of gold, lost many a well-loved comrade. And they fled away from the place of battle and saved their lives. Behind them, slain with spears and smitten with the sword-edge, their well-loved comrades, sons of princes, fell in death.

And the lord of Elam had the victory, and held the place of battle; and those who escaped the sword fled away to seek a stronghold. The foemen took their gold and sacked their splendid treasure-cities, Sodom

1975–2008

and Gomorrah. Women were torn from
their sheltering homes, widow and maid,
bereft of friends. And the foe led Abraham's kinsman captive out of the city of
Sodom, with all his substance. But truly
may we tell these war wolves' fate after
the battle, boasting their victory, leading
Lot captive away, and with him the goods
of the people and gold of the Southmen.

For a certain man who survived the
battle and the sword came running unto
Abraham, the Hebrew prince, and told him
the disaster, the fate of Lot, and how the
men of Sodom, and their strength, were
sorely smitten. And Abraham told these
tidings to his friends; the faithful man
besought his well-loved comrades, Aner
and Mamre and Eshcol, to bear him aid,
saying that it was grievous to his heart
and greatest of all sorrows, that his brother's
son should suffer thraldom. He bade those
valiant men devise a plan to free his kinsman, and his wife with him. And quickly the
three brothers spake, and healed the sorrow
of his heart with manful words, and pledged
their faith to Abraham to aid him, and
avenge his wrath upon his foes, or fall in
death.

Then the holy man bade his hearth-retainers take their weapons. Three hundred
and eighteen wielders of the ashen spear he
gathered, loyal-hearted men, of whom he

knew that each would stoutly bear his linden shield to battle. And Abraham went out, and the three earls who had pledged their faith, together with a great company of their people.[1] He would fain redeem his kinsman, Lot, from his distress. Brave were the warriors, stoutly bearing their bucklers upon the march. And when these war-wolves had journeyed nigh unto the camp, the son of Terah, wise of heart, bespake his captains (great was his need that they should wage grim war on either flank, and hard hand-play against the foe) and said that easily the Holy, Everlasting Lord could speed their fortunes in the spear-strife.

Then, in the shades of night, as I have heard, the warriors dared the battle. In the camp rose din of shields and spears, death of bowmen, crash of battle arrows. Bitterly the sharp spears pierced the hearts of men. In throngs their foemen, warriors and comrades, fell in death, where laughing they had borne away the spoil. And victory and glory of war forsook the strife of the Northmen. No twisted gold did Abraham offer in ransom for his brother's son, but battle; he smote and slew the foe in war. And the Lord of heaven smote in his behalf. Four armies fled, the kings and captains of the folk. Behind them lay the goodly host of hearth-retainers, cold in death, and in their track lay those who

[1] Grein: *him mid siðedon.*

sacked the homes of Sodom and Gomorrah, and bore away the young men and the gold. Lot's uncle gave them grim requital! And the lords of the army of Elam, shorn of their glory, continued in flight until they came nigh unto Damascus.

Then Abraham betook him to the track of their retreat, and beheld the flight of the foe. Lot was redeemed, and his possessions; the women returned with joy. Far and wide upon the field of slaughter the birds were tearing at the bodies of those foemen of the free. And Abraham brought the treasure of the Southmen, their wives and children, unto their homes again, and maidens to their kinsmen. Never did any man of living men with tiny band go forth more worthily to battle than those who rushed against that mighty host.

Southward the tidings of battle were borne to the people of Sodom: news of their fierce foes' flight. The lord of the folk, bereft of earls and desolate of friends, went out unto Abraham, to meet him. And with him journeyed Salem's treasure-warden, Melchizedek the mighty, the bishop of the folk. He came with gifts, gave Abraham fair greeting, the lord of armed men, and blessed him with God's blessing, and said:

"Well hast thou borne thee among men, before His eyes who gave thee glory in the battle—that is, God the Lord, who brake the power of thy foes, and let thee hew thy way to safety with the sword, regain the spoil, and fell thine enemies. They perished in the track of their retreat. The marching host throve not in battle, but God put them to flight. With His hands He shielded thee against the force of greater numbers in the battle because of the holy covenant which thou dost keep with the Lord of heaven."

And the prince laid his hand upon him and blessed him, and Abraham gave a tenth part of all the booty unto the bishop of God. Then unto Abraham spake the battle-king, the prince of Sodom, bereft of his warriors (he had need of favour):

"Restore me now the maidens of my people whom thou hast rescued with thy host from evil bondage. Keep thou the twisted gold that was my people's, the wealth and treasure. But let me lead again in freedom to their native land and wasted dwellings the children of my people, the women and lads and widows in their affliction. Our sons are dead and all our nobles, save a few only who must guard with me the marches of our land."

And straightway, crowned with valour and victory and glory, Abraham made answer before the earls. Right nobly spake he:

"I say to thee, O prince of men, before the Holy Lord of earth and heaven, there is no worldly treasure I will take, nor scot nor shilling of what I have redeemed for thee among the bowmen, great prince and lord of men, lest that thou afterward shouldest say that I grew rich with the riches of Sodom and its olden treasure. But thou mayest take hence with thee all that booty which I won for thee in battle, save only the portion of these lordly men, of Aner, and of Mamre, and of Eshcol. I will not willingly deprive these warriors of their right, for they upheld me in the shock of battle and fought to thine advantage. Depart now, taking home the well-wrought gold, and lovely maidens, the daughters of thy people. Thou needest not to dread the onrush of thy foes, or war of the Northmen, but the blood-stained birds of prey are resting on the mountain slopes, gorged with the slain of their armies."

Then the king departed to his home with the booty which the holy Hebrew prince, mindful of honour, had given him. And the Lord of heaven appeared again unto Abraham, comforting the noble man of heart with holy speech, and said:

"Great shall be thy reward! Let not thy heart be shaken, doing My will. Thou needest have no whit of dread if thou wilt keep My precepts, but I will shield thee with My hands, and shelter thee from every evil, so long as thy life endureth. Be not afraid."

And Abraham, full of years and noble deeds, made answer to his Lord and asked: "What comfort canst Thou give me, Lord of spirits, who am thus desolate? No need have I to heap up treasure for any child of mine, but after me my kinsmen shall enjoy my wealth. Thou grantest me no son, and therefore sorrow presseth on my heart. I can devise no counsel. My steward goeth to and fro rejoicing in his children, and firmly thinketh in his heart that after me his sons shall be my heirs. He seeth that no child is born to me."

And straightway God made answer unto him: "Never shall son of thy steward inherit thy goods; but thine own son shall have thy treasure when thy flesh lieth cold. Behold the heavens! Number their jewels, the shining stars, that shed their wondrous beauty far and wide, and blaze so brightly over the spacious sea. So shall thy tribe be and thy seed for number. Let not thy heart be troubled. Yet shall thy wife conceive and bear a son, great in goodness, to be warden of thy wealth, when thou art gone. Be not cast down. I am the Lord who, many a year ago, brought thee forth from out the land of the Chaldeans, with but a few, and gave thee this wide realm to rule. I give thee now My promise, prince of Hebrews, thy seed shall settle many a spacious kingdom, the regions of the world from the Egyptian borders even unto Euphrates, and where the Nile hems in a mighty land and the sea limits it. All this shall thy sons inhabit; each tract and tribal realm and lofty stone-built city, whatsoever those three waters and their foaming floods encircle with their streams."

Now Sarah's heart was heavy that she bare no goodly son to gladden Abraham; with bitter grief she spake unto her husband:

"The Lord of heaven hath denied me to increase thy tribe, or bear thee children under heaven. I have no hope that we shall have a son to stay our house. My heart is sad. My lord, do now according as I bid thee. Here is a virgin subject unto thee, a comely maid, a daughter of the Egyptian people. Bid her go quickly to thy bed, and thou shalt prove if by this woman the Lord will send an heir unto thy house."

And the blessed man gave ear unto the woman's counsels, and bade his handmaid go unto his bed, according as his wife had counselled him. And the maiden conceived by Abraham, and her heart grew arrogant. She stubbornly began to vex her mistress, was insolent, insulting, evil-hearted, and would not willingly be subject to her, but straightway entered into strife with Sarah. Then, as I have heard, the woman told her sorrow to her lord, speaking with bitter grief:

"Thou hast not done me right or justice! Since first my handmaid, Hagar, knew thy bed, according as I counselled thee, thou sufferest her to vex me day by day in word and deed. But her atonement shall be bitter if I may still rule over my own maid, dear Abraham. And may Almighty God, the Lord of lords, be judge between us."

And straightway Abraham, wise of heart, made answer: "Never will I let thee be dishonoured while we two live. But thou shalt deal with thine handmaid even according as it pleaseth thee."

Then was the wife of Abraham hard of heart and hostile-minded, ruthless, and merciless against her handmaid, and bitterly declared her hate. And the maiden fled from thraldom and oppression, and would not brook punishment or retribution for what she wrought against Sarah. But she fled into the wilderness. And there a thane of glory, an angel of the Lord, found her sad of heart and questioned her:

"Whither art thou hastening, unhappy girl, handmaid of Sarah?"

And straightway she answered him: "Devoid of all good things, in misery, I fled away out of my dwelling, from the hate of my lady, from injury and wrong. Here in the wilderness with tear-stained face I shall abide my doom, when from my heart grim hunger or the wolf shall tear my soul and sorrow."

And the angel answered her: "Seek not to flee away and leave thy lord, but return again, deserve honour, be of humble heart, constant in virtue, and faithful to thy lord. Thou, Hagar, shalt bring forth a son to Abraham. And I say unto thee that men shall call him Ishmael. He shall be terrible, and swift to war; his hand shall be against the tribes of men, his kinsmen. Many shall war upon him bitterly. And from that prince shall spring a race and an unnumbered tribe. Return again to seek thy lord, and dwell with them that have thee in possession."

And she hearkened unto the angel's counsel, and returned again unto her lord, according as the holy messenger of God commanded in words of wisdom. And Abraham had lived for six-and-eighty winters in the world when Ishmael was born. And the boy grew strong and throve according as the angel, the faithful minister of peace, had told the maid. And after thirteen years the Lord, Eternal God, said unto Abraham:

"Dearest of men, keep well our covenant as I shall show thee, and I will prosper thee and honour thee in every season. Be swift to work My will. I will be mindful of the covenant and pledge I gave thee to thy comfort, because thy soul was sad. Thou shalt sanctify thy household, and set a victor-sign on every male, if thou wilt have in Me a lord or faithful friend unto thy people. I will be lord and shepherd of this folk if ye will serve Me in your hearts, and keep My laws. And each male child that cometh into the world, among this people, shall be devoted unto Me in seven nights' time, by the victor-token, or else cut off from all the world with persecution, and exiled from all good.

"Do as I bid thee; I will be gracious unto you if ye will use that token of true faith. Thy wife shall bear a son, and men shall call him Isaac. Thou shalt not need to shame thee for him, but I will grant him grace divine, by My great might, and many a friend. He shall receive My blessing and My bliss, My love and favour. From him shall spring a mighty people and many a valiant leader, rulers of kingdoms, lords of the world, renowned afar."

Then Abraham laid his face upon the ground and pondered these sayings in his heart with scorn. For he deemed that never the day would come when Sarah, his grey-haired wife, would bear a son. Full well he knew that she had lived an hundred winters in the world. And full of years he spake unto the Lord:

"May Ishmael live according to Thy laws, O Lord, and render Thee a thankful and a steadfast spirit, an earnest heart to do Thy will, by night and day, in word and deed."

And graciously Eternal God, Almighty Lord, made answer:

"Yet shall Sarah bear a son, though old

in winters, and fate shall be fulfilled according to My word. I will bless Ishmael, thy firstborn, with My blessing as thou dost ask, that his days may be long in the land, and his race may multiply. This will I grant thee. So also will I prosper Isaac, thy younger son, who is not yet born, with every good and pleasant thing all the days of his life. And I will surely keep My covenant with him and holy faith, and show him favour."

And Abraham did even as Eternal God commanded, and, in accordance with his Lord's behest, he set the sign of the covenant upon his son, and bade his bondmen also bear that holy token. He was wise of heart, and mindful of the covenant and pledge which God had given him; and he himself received the glorious sign. God, the Mighty King, increased his glory in the world. And he strove in all his ways to work the will of his Lord. . . .

But the woman laughed at the Lord of hosts with derision; full of years, she pondered those sayings in her heart with scorn. She had no faith that His words would be fulfilled. And when the Lord of heaven heard that in her bower the wife of Abraham laughed in unbelief, then spake the Holy God:

"Lo! Sarah trusteth not My word. Yet all shall be fulfilled according as I promised thee in the beginning. I tell thee truly, at this self-same season thy wife shall bear a son. And when I come again unto this dwelling My word shall be fulfilled, and thine eyes shall behold thy son, dear Abraham."

And after these words they departed swiftly away from the place of oracle. The holy spirits turned their steps (and the Prince of light was their companion) till they beheld high Sodom's city-walls. They saw high halls towering above precious treasure and mansions above ruddy gold. And the Righteous Lord of heaven held long discourse with Abraham :

"I hear loud tumult in this city and brawling of sinful men, the boastful words of tipplers drunk with ale, and evil speech of multitudes within their walls. Heavy are the sins of this people and the offences of these faithless men. But I will search out what this people do, O Hebrew prince, and whether they sin so greatly in their thoughts and deeds as their evil tongues speak fraud and guile. Verily brimstone and black flame, bitter and grim and fiercely burning, shall visit vengeance on these heathen folk." . . .

And so these men abode their punishment and woe within their walls, and their wives with them. Proud in their strength, they repaid God evil for good until the Lord of spirits, Prince of life and light, could no longer withhold His wrath. Stern of heart, God sent two mighty messengers among them

who came at even-tide unto the city of Sodom.
They came upon a man sitting in the gate of
the city, even the son of Haran, and they
appeared as young men before the eyes of
the sage. Then the servant of the Lord
arose and went unto the strangers, and
greeted them with kindness; he was mindful
of what is right and fitting among men, and
offered them a shelter for the night. And
the noble messengers of God made answer:

"We thank thee for the favour thou hast
showed us. Yet do we think to bide here
quietly beside this street until the time of the
dawn, when God shall send again the sun."

Then Lot fell at their feet, and knelt upon
the ground [1] before his guests, and offered
them food and rest, the shelter of his house,
and entertainment. And they accepted the
kindness of the prince with thanks, and went
in quickly with him unto his dwelling as the
Hebrew earl pointed them the way. And the
lordly hero, wise of heart, gave them fair
entertainment in his hall, until the evening
light vanished away. Then night came, hard
upon the heels of day, and clothed the ocean-
streams with darkness, and all the glory of
the world, seas and wide-stretching land.

Then in great throngs the dwellers of
Sodom, young and old, undear to God, came
to demand the strangers, in multitudes
encompassed Lot about, and his guests.

---

[1] Grein: *feoll on foldan.*

They bade him lead the holy heralds out from the lofty hall into their power. Shamelessly they said that they would know these men. Of decency they had no heed. Then swiftly Lot arose, deviser of counsel, and went forth from his dwelling; the son of Haran, mindful of wisdom, spake unto all that gathering of men:

"Within my house two stainless daughters dwell. (Neither of them yet has known a man.) Do now as I bid you and forsake this sin. Them will I give you rather than that ye work this shame against your nature, and grievous evil against the sons of men. Take now the maidens and leave my guests in peace, for I will defend them against you before God, if so I may."

And all that multitude of godless men with one accord made answer unto him: "This seemeth meet and very right: that thou leave this land! An exile, from afar thou camest to this country, desolate of friends, and lacking food. And now wilt thou be judge over us, if so may be, and teach our people?"

Then, as I have heard, the heathen leaders laid hand on Lot and seized him. But his guests, the righteous strangers, brought him aid, and drew him within his dwelling from out the clutches of these cruel men. And straightway the eyes of all those standing round about were darkened; and suddenly the host of city-dwellers became blind. They might not storm the halls, with savage hearts against the strangers, as they strove to do, but stoutly the ministers of God withstood them. Lot's guests had sturdy strength, and smote the host with vengeance. Fairly the faithful ministers of peace spake unto Lot :

"If thou have any son, or kinsman dear among this people, or any friend of these maidens whom we here behold, lead forth in haste from the city those dear to thee, and save thy life, lest thou too perish with these faithless men. Because of the sins of Sodom and Gomorrah the Lord hath bidden give them over to fire and black flame, to smite the people in their dwellings with the pangs of death, and work His vengeance. The hour is nigh at hand. Flee upon the paths of earth, and save thy life. To thee the Lord is gracious." . . .

And straightway Lot made answer unto them : "I may not wander so far hence, afoot, in search of safety, with these women. But ye may fairly show me love and friendship, and grant me grace and favour. I know a little high-built town not far from here ; there grant me rest and respite, in Zoar to find safety. If ye will shield that lofty stronghold from the flame, we may abide there for a time secure, and save our lives."

And friendly was the righteous angels' answer: "Thou shalt receive this boon, since thou hast spoken of the city. Go quickly to that stronghold, and we will grant thee peace and our protection. We will not wreak God's vengeance on these faithless men, nor slay this sinful race, till thou hast brought thy children unto Zoar, and thy wife with them."

Then Abraham's kinsman hastened to the stronghold. He swiftly journeyed with his women, and stayed not foot until he led his children into Zoar, under the city-gates, and his wife with them. And when the sun arose, peace-candle of men, then, as I have heard, the Lord of glory sent brimstone out of heaven, black fire and raging flame, in vengeance upon men, because so long in days gone by they had displeased the Lord. The Ruler of spirits gave them their reward!

And a great fear gripped the heathen race; din arose in their cities, wailing of sinful men, a wretched people at the point of death. All that was green in the golden cities the flame devoured; likewise no little portion of the wide land round about was covered with flame and terror. Fair groves and fruits of the earth were turned to ash and glowing ember, even as far as that grim vengeance swept the broad land of men. A roaring flame, destroying all things high and spacious, consumed the wealth of Sodom and Gomorrah.

All this the Lord God destroyed, and the people with it.

But when Lot's wife heard the rushing flame, and dying men within the city, she looked behind her to that place of death. Straightway, the writings tell us, she was changed into the likeness of a pillar of salt; and ever since, the image (far-famed is the story) has stood in silence where that bitter vengeance came upon her, because she would not heed the bidding of the thanes of glory. Hard and high-towering in that spot of earth she must abide her fate, the doom of God, till time shall cease and the world vanish away. That is a wonder which the Lord of glory wrought!

And Abraham, the man of wisdom, went out alone at dawn and came again unto the place where he had spoken with his Lord. Far and wide he saw the fatal smoke curling upward from the earth. Pride had come upon that people and drunkenness, and they became too insolent in evil and bold in sin. God's judgments they forgot, and truth, and Him who gave them wealth and blessing in their cities. Wherefore the Prince of angels sent a consuming flame in punishment upon them. But our Faithful Lord was gracious, and remembered Abraham, His beloved, as oft He did, and delivered Lot, his kinsman, when the multitude were slain. Now Lot, the valiant, durst no longer dwell in that stronghold for fear of God, but he departed out of the city, and his children with him, to seek a dwelling far from the place of slaughter, and found, at last, a cave upon the slope of a high hill. And Lot, the blessed, dear unto God and faithful, abode there many a day, and his two daughters with him. . . .

Thus did they, and the elder daughter went in first unto their father's bed, as he lay drunk with wine. And the old man knew not when the maidens came unto his bed, but his mind and wit were clouded within him, and, drunk with wine, he knew not the coming of the maids. And the lovely sisters conceived, and bare sons unto their aged father. Lot's older daughter called her son's name Moab. And the younger called her son's name Ammon, as the sacred writings say. Of these princes sprang a countless folk, two famous peoples. One tribe men call the Moabites, a far-famed race; the other tribe men call the Ammonites.

Then the brother of Haran departed with his wife and household and with all his substance to be subject unto Abimelech. And Abraham said unto men, of Sarah, his wife, "She is my sister," and thereby saved his life. For well he knew he had few friends or kinsfolk among that people. And the prince sent forth his thanes and bade them bring him Abraham's wife.[1]

---

[1] Grein: *bryde Abrahames*.

Then a second time, while dwelling among alien people, Abraham's wife was taken from her husband, and given into a stranger's arms. But the Eternal Lord sustained them as He oft had done. Our Saviour came at night unto the king as he lay drunk with wine. The King of truth spake unto the prince in a dream, and in anger denounced him:

"The wife of Abraham hast thou taken from him, and for this deed of evil death shall smite thy soul within thy breast."

And, heavy with feasting, the lord of sin began to speak in his slumber: "O Prince of angels, wilt Thou ever, in Thine anger, suffer a life to fail which liveth with righteous ways and upright heart, and seeketh mercy at Thy hands? I questioned not the woman, but she said that she was Abraham's sister. And I have wrought no evil against her, nor any sin."

Then again a second time the Righteous Lord, Eternal God, spake unto him in his dream, and said: "O prince of men, if thou reck aught of longer living in the world, restore this woman unto Abraham to be his wife. He is wise and righteous, and may behold the King of glory and speak with Him. But thou shalt perish with thy goods and treasure, if thou withhold this woman from the prince. But if that just and patient man will intercede for thee, he may prevail with

Me to let thee live unharmed, enjoying blessings, friends, and treasure all the days of thy life."

Then in fear the warden of the people awoke from his slumber, and bade summon his counsellors. Smitten with terror, Abimelech told them the words of God. And they feared God's vengeance on that deed, according to the dream. Then the king in haste called Abraham before him. The mighty prince said unto him:

"Tell me now what evil I have done thee, Hebrew prince, since first thou camest to our land with thy possessions, that now so fiercely thou shouldest lay a snare before me. Lo, Abraham! a stranger to this people, thou wouldest entrap us, and defile with sin. Thou saidest Sarah was thy sister and thy kin! Through her thou wouldest have done me grievous hurt and endless evil. We harboured thee with honour, in friendly wise allotting thee a dwelling in this realm, and lands for thine enjoyment. But in no friendly way dost thou reward or thank us for our favours."

And Abraham answered: "I did it not in guile or hatred, nor yet to work thee any woe. But I was far from mine own people, prince of men, and shielded me by craft from violence and death. Since Holy God first led me forth of old from the home of my lord and father, desolate of friends, I have visited many a people, many an alien race, and this woman with me. And ever this fear was in my heart, seeing I was a stranger, lest some foe should slay me, and take this woman to himself. Wherefore I said that Sarah was my sister, and this I told the war-smiths everywhere on earth where we two homeless needs must dwell [1] with strangers. And so I did in this land also, mighty prince, when I came under thy protection. I knew not if the fear of God Almighty was among this people, when first I came here. Therefore, with care, I hid from thee and from thy thanes the truth, that Sarah was my wife and shared my bed."

Then Abimelech began to endow Abraham with treasure, and gave him his wife again; and because he had taken his wife he gave him, to boot, wandering herds and servants [2] and gleaming silver. And the lord of men said also unto Abraham:

"Abide with us and choose thee a dwelling in this land, and an abode whereso it pleaseth thee; thee must I keep. Be thou a faithful friend, and we will give thee riches."

And the dispenser of treasure spake also unto Sarah, and said: "No need hath Abraham, thy lord, to reproach thee, O maiden of elfin beauty, because thou hast trod my halls. With gleaming silver will I make requital for this wrong. Care not to

[1] Grein 2: *wunian* for *winnan*.   [2] Grein: *weorcðeos*.

go forth from this folk-land, seeking elsewhere unknown friends, but dwell ye here."

And Abraham did according to the bidding of the prince, accepting the friendship offered by his lord, with love and favour. Dear was he unto God; knowing great blessedness and peace, and walking in his Lord's protection and under the shelter of His wings, so long as his life endured.

Yet was God still angered against Abimelech for the wrong he had wrought against Sarah and against Abraham, in severing the bonds of these beloved, man and wife. He suffered woe and bitter punishment; the maidens, slave nor free, might not bear children to their lords, but God denied them, till holy Abraham prayed his Lord, Eternal God, for mercy. And the Lord of angels granted him his prayer, and for the king restored fertility to man and maid, to slave and free. The Lord of heaven suffered again their number to increase, their riches and possessions; and the Almighty Warden of mankind was merciful of heart unto Abimelech, as Abraham besought Him.

Then the Almighty Lord came unto Sarah, according to His word; our God, the Lord of life, fulfilled His promise to His dear ones, the man and woman. His wife brought forth a son to Abraham, and, ere his mother had conceived him, the Prince of angels called him Isaac. And Abraham with his own hand set the glorious sign upon him within the week his mother bare him. And the boy grew strong and throve, and his nature was noble. Now Abraham had lived an hundred winters in the world when his wife, with thankful heart, brought forth a son. And he had waited long for that event since first the Lord, by His own word, announced the day of joy.

And it came to pass upon a time that the woman saw Ishmael playing before Abraham as they sat with holy hearts at meat together, and all their household drank and revelled. Then said his wife, the noble woman, to her lord:

"Beloved lord, and warden of treasure, grant me a boon! Bid Hagar go forth from among us, and Ishmael with her. No longer shall we dwell together, if I may rule and have my will. Never shall Ishmael, after thee, divide the heritage with Isaac, my son, when thou hast given up the ghost from out thy body."

Then it grieved Abraham in his heart that he must drive his own son into exile; but God, the Just and Righteous, succoured him. He knew that the heart of the man was heavy with sorrow. The King of angels, the Eternal Lord, said unto Abraham:

"Let care and sorrow vanish from thy heart, and hearken unto the woman, thy wife. Bid Hagar go forth from this land,

and Ishmael, the lad, with her. And I will multiply his race, and stablish them with ample blessings, as I have promised by My word."

And the man hearkened unto his Lord, and drove them forth in sadness from his dwelling, the woman and his son. . . .

"Clear is it that the Just God, Lord of heaven, is with thee, granting thee triumph by His might and wisdom, and strengthening thy heart with grace divine. Therefore ye throve in all your dealings, with friend or foe, in word or deed. With His hands the Lord God prospered thee in all thy ways. That is full widely known unto the city-dwellers! Graciously grant me now, I pray thee, Hebrew prince, thy promise and thy pledge, that thou wilt be a faithful friend to me, according to the kindness I have done thee since, wretched and in exile, thou camest from afar unto this land. Requite it now with kindness that I grudged thee not of land or favour. Be gracious to this nation, my people, if the Lord our God, who ruleth the fates of men, will grant thee to extend the borders of this people, dealing out wealth to warriors of the shield, and treasure to the brave."

And Abraham gave a pledge unto Abimelech that he would do according to his prayer. And the Hebrew prince, the blessed son of Terah, abode a long time in the land

of the Philistines, wretched and in exile.
And the Lord of angels assigned him a
dwelling-place, and the city-dwelling sons
of men call that land Beersheba. There
the holy man built a lofty city wherein to
dwell, and planted a grove and raised an
altar, and on the altar made ample offerings
and sacrifice to God, who granted him life
and blessing under heaven.

Then the Mighty Lord made a trial of
the prince, and proved his strength, and
sternly spake unto him, saying:

"Abraham! Betake thee quickly on a
journey, and with thee lead thine only son.
Thou shalt offer thy son Isaac unto Me in
sacrifice. When thou hast mounted the
steep downs and the slope of the high land
which I will show thee, there shalt thou
build an altar, and kindle a flame, slay
thy son with the sword, and burn his body
with black flame, and offer it a sacrifice
to Me."

He delayed not the journey, but swiftly
made him ready. For the word of the Lord
of angels was terrible to him, and his Lord
was dear. The blessed Abraham rested not
nor slept nor spurned his Lord's behest, but
the holy man girded him with a grey sword,
and showed that fear of the Lord of spirits
abode in his heart. The aged dispenser of
gold began to saddle his asses, and bade two
young men journey with him; his son was

2834-2868

the third, and he the fourth. And he went out from his house with Isaac, the lad, according as God commanded. He went with speed and hastened on the paths of earth, according as the Lord marked out the way across the waste, until, in gleaming glory, the dawn of the third day arose over the deep water.

Then the blessed man beheld the high hills towering up, as the Lord of heaven had told him. And Abraham said unto his servants:

"Abide ye here in this place, and we two will come again, when we have worshipped God."

And the prince and his son departed across the weald to the place which the Lord had showed him; the lad carried wood, and the father bare fire and sword. And the lad, young in winters, spake unto Abraham and said:

"Here have we fire and sword, my lord! But where is the fair burnt-offering thou thinkest to sacrifice to God?"

And Abraham answered (firm was his resolve to do as God had bidden): "That will the Righteous Lord, the Warden of mankind, provide as seemeth right to Him."

Stout of heart he mounted the high downs, and his son with him, according as Eternal God commanded, until he stood upon the ridge of the high land in the place¹ which the Firm and Faithful Lord had showed him. And there he built a pyre and kindled a flame and bound his son, hand and foot, and laid Isaac, the lad, on the altar, and seized his sword by the hilt. With his own hand he would have slain him, and quenched the flame with the blood of his son.

Then a thane of God, an angel from on high, called unto Abraham with a loud voice. In stillness he abode the herald's message and answered the angel. Swiftly the glorious minister of God addressed him from the heavens:

"Slay not thy son, dear Abraham, but take the lad from the altar alive. The God of glory is gracious unto him! Great shall thy reward be, Hebrew prince, true meed of victory and ample gifts, at the holy hands of the Heavenly King. The Lord of spirits will bless thee with His blessing because His love and favour were dearer unto thee than thine own son."

The altar-fire stood kindled. The Lord of men had gladdened the heart of Abraham, kinsman of Lot, when He restored to him his son, alive. And the blessed man, brother of Haran, looked over his shoulder and beheld a ram standing not far off, caught fast in the brambles. And Abraham took it, and laid it upon the altar in the stead of his

[1] Supplying *stowe*.

son, and drawing his sword made ready an offering and an altar smoking with the blood of the ram, and sacrificed that offering to God, and gave Him thanks for all the loving-kindness which the Lord had showed him, early and late.

EXODUS

EXODUS

Lo! far and wide throughout the earth we have heard how the laws of Moses, a wondrous code, proclaim to men reward of heavenly life for all the blessed after death, and lasting gain for every living soul. Let him hear who will!

On him the Lord of hosts, the Righteous King, showed honour in the wilderness, and the Eternal Ruler gave him might to work great wonders. He was beloved of God, a lord of men, a wise and ready leader of the host, a bold folk-captain. Affliction came upon the tribe of Pharaoh, the enemy of God, when the Lord of victories entrusted to the bold folk-leader his kinsmen's lives, and gave the sons of Abraham a dwelling and an habitation. Great was his reward! The Lord was gracious unto him and gave him weapon-might against the terror of his foes, wherewith he overcame in battle many a warrior, and the strength of hostile men.

And first the Lord of hosts spake unto him and told him many wonders, how the Triumphant Lord in wisdom wrought the world, and the compass of the earth, and the arching heavens; and told His own name, which the sons of men, wise patriarchs of old, knew not before, though they knew many things. And the Lord honoured the leader of the host, the foe of Pharaoh, and strengthened him with righteous strength on his departure, when, of old, in punishment that mighty host was drenched with death.

Wailing arose at the fall of their princes; their hall-joys were hushed and their treasure was scattered. Fiercely at midnight He smote the oppressors, slaying their firstborn, laying their watchmen low. Wide the destroyer's path, and the way of the fell folk-slayer! The whole land mourned the dead. The host departed. Loud was the voice of their wailing, little their joy! Locked were the hands of the laughter-makers; the multitude had leave to go its way, a wandering folk. The Fiend was robbed and all the hosts of hell. Heaven's might came upon them; their idols fell. That was a glorious day through all the world when the host went forth! Many a year the vile Egyptians suffered bondage, because they thought for ever to refuse to Moses' kinsmen, if God would let them, their longing for the journey of their heart's desire.

The host was ready. The prince who led them was stalwart and bold. He passed by many a stronghold with his people, leaders and lands of many hostile men, by narrow, lonely paths and unknown ways, until at last they marched, in armour, against the

Ethiopian realm. Their lands were covered with a cloud, their border-homes upon the mountain-slopes. Past these, with many a hindrance, Moses led his people. And two nights after they escaped their foes God bade the noble prince to make encampment about the town of Etham in the marchlands, with all his force, a mighty army, and tumult of the host.

With anxious hearts they hastened on their northward way; they knew that southward lay the Ethiop's land, parched hill-slopes and a race burned brown by the heat of the sun. But Holy God shielded that folk against the fiery heat, stretching a covering over the flaming heavens, and over the burning air a holy veil. A cloud widestretching severed earth from heaven, and led the host; burning and heavenly bright the fiery flame was quenched. The warriors marvelled, most joyous of hosts. The shelter of the day-shield moved across the heavens; God in His wisdom had covered the course of the sun with a sail, though earth-dwelling men knew not the mast-ropes, nor might behold the yards, nor understand the way in which that greatest of tents was fastened. So He showed honour and glory upon the faithful!

Then was a third encampment to the comfort of the folk. The army all beheld the holy sail, the gleaming marvel of the sky, towering above them. And all that folk, the men of Israel, perceived that there the Lord of hosts was present to measure out a camp. Before them moved two columns in the heavens, fire and cloud, sharing alike the service of the Holy Spirit, the journey of brave-hearted men, by day and night.

And in the dawn, as I have heard, the valiant-hearted blared forth their trumpet-calls, in peals of thunder. And all the host, the band of the brave, arose and made them ready, according as Moses, their glorious leader, gave bidding to God's people. They beheld their guide go forth before them measuring out the path of life. The sail governed their journey, and after it, with joyful hearts, the seamen trod their path through the great waters.

Loud was the tumult of the host. Each evening rose a heavenly beacon, a second wondrous marvel after the setting of the sun, a pillar of flame shining in splendour over the hosts of men. Bright were its shining beams above the warriors; their bucklers gleamed, the shadows vanished away. No secret place could hide the deep night-shadows. Heaven's candle burned. Needs must this new night warden watch above the host, lest in the stormy weather grey heath and desert-terror should overcome their souls with sudden fear. Streaming locks of fire had their guide, and shining beams, menacing the host with flame and terror, and threatening destruction to that people in the waste, except they swiftly hearkened unto Moses. Armour gleamed, and bucklers glistened as the warriors took their steadfast way. And over the troops and high above the host stood the banner, moving as they moved, even unto the stronghold of the sea at the land's end. And there they pitched a camp and rested, for they were weary. Stewards brought the warriors food and strengthened them. And when the trumpet sang they stretched themselves upon the hills, shipmen within their tents. That was the fourth encampment and pause of the shield-men by the Red Sea.

There dread tidings of inland pursuit came unto the army. A great fear fell upon them, and dread of the host. So the exiles abode the coming of the fierce pursuers, who long had crushed those homeless men and wrought them injury and woe. They heeded not the covenant which the ancient king had given [1] aforetime, who became the people's heir and had their treasure, and greatly throve. All this the Egyptian race forgot when their wrath was stirred by a quarrel. They wrought great wrong to Moses' kinsmen, broke the covenant, and slew them. Their hearts were filled with faithlessness and rage, the mighty passions of men. They

[1] Grein: *getiðode*.

would fain requite the gift of life with evil, that the people of Moses might pay for that day's work in blood, if Mighty God would prosper their destructive journey.

Then the hearts of the earls were hopeless within them as they beheld the shining bands, the hosts of Pharaoh, marching from out the south, uplifting a forest of lances, with banners waving above them, a great host treading the border-paths. Their spears were in array, shields gleamed and trumpets sang; the battle line rolled on. Over dead bodies circling screamed the birds of battle, dewy-feathered, greedy for war, dark carrion-lovers. In hope of food, the wolves, remorseless beasts of slaughter, sang a grim evening-song; dogging the march of the foe, they abode the coming of death; the march warders howled in the midnight. The doomed soul fled; the host was compassed about.

Now and again the proud thanes of the host measured the mile-paths on their steeds. The prince of men rode forth before the troops, the war-king raised the standard; the battle-warden bound on helm and chin-guard (banners gleamed) in expectation of war, shook his armour, and bade his warlike host, his firm-ranked cohorts, go boldly into battle. The foe beheld with hostile eyes the coming of the landsmen. About him fearless fighters moved; grey wolves of war went forward to the onslaught thirsting for battle, loyal of heart. He chose the flower of his people for that service, two thousand far-famed heroes of high birth, kings and kinsmen. And each led out his men, and all the warriors that he well could muster in the appointed time. The young men were gathered together, the kings in their pomp. Frequently sounding, the well-known voice of the horn signalled the host where the war-troop of heroes should bear their arms. So the dark horde was marshalled; throng after throng, in thousands, hasted thither, a countless host. They were resolved, in vengeance for their brothers, to slay the tribes of Israel with the sword, at the break of day.

Then a sound of wailing arose in the camp, an evening-song of woe. A great fear was upon them; the nets of death encompassed them about. The fatal tidings flew abroad; tumult arose. The foe were resolute, a horde in armour gleaming, until the mighty angel who upheld that host scattered the proud and hateful multitude, so that no more might one behold another's face; but their journey was divided.

All that long night the fugitives had respite, though foes beset them upon either hand, on the one side that great host, on the other side the sea. They had no way of escape nor any hope of their inheritance, but halted on the hills in shining armour with foreboding of ill. And all the band of kinsmen watched and waited for the coming of the greater host until the dawn, when Moses bade the earls with brazen trumpets muster the folk, bade warriors rise and don their coats of mail, bear shining arms, take thought on valour, and summon the multitude with signal-beacons unto the sandy shore of the sea.

The leaders bold obeyed the battle-signal; the host made ready. The seamen heard the trumpet-summons, and struck their tents upon the hills. The army was astir. They numbered off twelve companies of valiant men to form the van of battle against their foes' grim wrath. The host was in an uproar. From every noble tribe among that people were chosen fifty cohorts, under shield, the flower of the folk. And every cohort of that famous army was of a thousand warriors, far-famed wielders of the spear.

That was a warlike band. The leaders of the army welcomed not among that number the weak, who yet because of youth could not defend them under board and byrnie against a wily foe, who never yet had known the baleful thrust, the bitter wound, the insolent play of the spear over the edge of the linden shield. Nor might the aged, grey-haired warriors be of service in the battle if their strength had failed them. But according to their strength they joined the fray, even according as their valour would endure with honour among men, and their strength suffice to undergo the spear-strife.[1] The army of these sturdy men was mustered, and ready to advance. Their banner rose on high, a gleaming column, and all abode there nigh unto the sea until their guiding beacon pierced the clouds, and shone upon their linden shields.

Then a herald rose before the warriors, a valiant leader, and, lifting up his shield, he bade the captains of the host make silence, that all the multitude might hear the words of their brave lord. The shepherd of the kingdom fain would speak with holy voice unto his legions. The leader of the host in words of worth addressed them :

"Be not afraid though Pharaoh leadeth hither this mighty host of sword-men, a multitude of earls. Upon them all this day Almighty God will give requital by my hand, that they may live no longer to vex the tribes of Israel with woe. Ye shall not dread doomed armies and dead men. Their fleeting life hath run unto the end. The knowledge of God hath vanished from your hearts. I give you better counsel, to serve the God of glory, and pray the Lord of life for victory and grace and safety, wherever ye may journey. He is the Eternal God of Abraham, Creation's Lord, magnanimous and mighty,

[1] Grein : *gegan mihte*.

who with His strong hand guardeth all this host."

Then the lord of men spake with a loud voice before the multitude and said: "Look now, dearest of people, with your eyes and behold a marvel! In my right hand grasping this green rod I smote the ocean depths. The waves rise up; the waters form a rampart-wall. The sea is thrust aside. The ways are dry: grey army-roads, ancient foundations (never have I heard in all the world that men before set foot thereon), shining plains, imprisoned deep sea-bottoms over which of old the great waves foamed. The south wind, breath of the ocean, hath driven them back. The sea is cleft asunder; the ebbing waters spewed up sand. Well I know Almighty God hath showed you mercy, ye bronze-clad earls. Most haste is best now, that ye may escape the clutch of foes since God hath reared a rampart of the red sea-streams. These walls are fairly builded to the roof of heaven, a wondrous wave-road."

And after these words the multitude arose, the host of the valiant. The sea lay tranquil. Upon the sand the legions raised their standards and shining linden shields. And over against the Israelites the wall of water stood firm and upright for the space of one whole day. Of one mind was that company of earls. The wall of water [1] shielded them with

---
[1] Grein: *ẏða weall.*

sure defence. In no wise did they scorn their holy leader's counsels as the time for deeds drew near, when the words of their well-loved lord were ended, and the voice of his eloquence was still.

The fourth tribe led the way, a throng of warriors, marching through the sea upon the green sea-bottom. The tribe of Judah trod that unknown road alone, before their kinsmen, and God Almighty gave them great reward for that day's work, granting them glory of triumphant deeds, that they might have dominion over kingdoms and sway their kinsmen. As they descended on the ocean-bottom that mighty tribe had lifted up their standard mid the spear-host, high above their shields their battle ensign, a golden lion, bravest of beasts. Not long would they endure oppression by the lord of any people while they might live and lift their spears to battle. In the van were strife and stubborn hand-play, warriors valiant in the weapon-struggle, fearless fighters, bloody wounds and clash of helmets, onrush of a battle-host, as Judah's sons advanced.

Behind that army proudly marched the seamen, sons of Reuben; the vikings bore their bucklers over the salt sea-marsh, a multitude of men, a mighty legion, advancing unafraid. For his sin's sake Reuben yielded his dominion and marched behind his kinsmen. From him his brother took his right as first-born in the tribe, his eminence and wealth. Yet was he ready.

And after them with thronging bands the sons of Simeon marched, the third division. Banners waved above the marching warriors; with flashing spears the battle troop pressed on. Over the ocean's bosom [1] dawn arose, God's beacon, radiant morning. The multitude went forth, the host advanced, one mail-clad band behind another. And one man only led this mighty folk, tribe after tribe, upon their march beneath the pillar of cloud, whereby he won renown. And each observed the right of nations and the rank of earls, as Moses gave them bidding.

One father had they all, one of the patriarchs, a well-loved leader, wise of heart and dear unto his kinsmen, who held the land-right and begat a line of valiant men, the tribe of Israel, a holy race, God's own peculiar people. So ancient writers tell us in their wisdom, who best have known the lineage of men, their kinship and descent.

Noah, the great prince, sailed over unknown waters, deepest of floods that ever came on earth, and his three sons with him. Within his heart he cherished holy faith. Wherefore he steered across the ocean-streams the richest treasure whereof I ever heard. To save the life of all the tribes of earth the wise sea-prince had numbered

---

[1] Grein: *begong*.

out a lasting remnant, a first generation, male and female, of every living kind that brought forth offspring, more various than men now know. And likewise in the bosom of their ship they bore the seed of every growing thing that men enjoy beneath the heavens.

Now Abraham's father, as the wise men tell us, was ninth from Noah in lineage and descent. This is the Abraham the God of angels named with a name, and gave the holy tribes into his keeping, far and near, and made him mighty over nations. He lived in exile. Thereafter, at the Holy One's behest, he took the lad, most dear of all to him, and they two, son and father, climbed together a high land unto the hill of Sion. And there, so men have heard, they found a covenant and holy pledge, and saw God's glory. And there, in after years, the son of David, the great king, the wisest of all earthly princes, according to the teaching of the prophets, built a temple unto God, a holy fane, the holiest and highest and most famous among men, the greatest and most splendid of all temples the sons of men have built upon the earth.

Abraham took Isaac, his son, and went to the place appointed, and kindled the altar flame. The first of murderers was not more doomed. As a bequest to men he would have sacrificed his well-loved son with fire and flame, his only heir on earth, the best of children, the lasting hope and comfort of his life, for which he long had waited. The far-famed man laid hand upon the lad and drew his ancient sword (loud rang the blade), and showed he held his son's life not more dear than to obey the King of heaven. Up rose the earl. He would have slain his son, and put the lad to death with blood-red blade, if God had not withheld him. The Glorious Father would not take his son in holy sacrifice, but laid His hand upon him. And out of heaven a restraining Voice, a Voice of glory, spake, and said to him:

"Abraham! Put not the lad, thy son, to death, nor slay him with the sword! The Lord of all hath proven thee, and truth is known, that thou hast kept the covenant with God, a faithful compact. And that shall be to thee an everlasting peace through all the days of thy life for ever. Doth the son of man require a greater pledge? Heaven and earth may not cover the words of His glory, which are ampler and greater than the regions of earth may include, the orb of the world, and the heavens above, the ocean depths and the murmuring air. The King of angels and Wielder of fates, Lord of hosts, Dispenser of victory, sweareth an oath by His life, that men on earth with all their wisdom shall never know the number of thy tribe and kinsmen, shield-bearing men, to tell it truly, except someone shall grow so wise of heart that he alone may number all the stones on earth and stars in heaven, sand of the sea-dunes, and salt waves of the sea. But thy tribe, the best of peoples, free-born of their fathers, shall dwell in the land of Canaan between the two seas even unto the nations of Egypt." . . .

Then all that folk was smitten with terror; fear of the flood fell on their wretched hearts. The great sea threatened death. The sloping hills were soaked with blood; the sea spewed gore. In the deep was uproar, the waves were filled with weapons; a death-mist rose. The Egyptians turned and fled away in fear, perceiving their peril. They were shaken with horror and fain to reach their homes. Their boasting was humbled. The dreadful rushing sea swept over them. Nor did any of that army come ever again to their homes, but Fate cut off retreat and locked them in the sea.

Where before lay open roads the ocean raged. The host was overwhelmed. The seas flowed forth; an uproar rose to heaven, a moan of mighty legions. There rose a great cry of the doomed, and over them the air grew dark. Blood dyed the deep. The walls of water were shattered; the greatest of sea-deaths lashed the heavens. Brave princes died in throngs. At the sea's end hope of return had vanished away. War-shields flashed. The wall of water, the mighty sea-stream, rushed over the heroes. The multitude was fettered fast in death, deprived of escape, cunningly bound. The ocean-sands awaited the doom ordained when the flowing billows, the ice-cold, wandering sea with its salt waves, a naked messenger of ill, a hostile warrior smiting down its foes, should come again to seek its ancient bed.

The blue air was defiled with blood. The roaring ocean menaced the march of the seamen with terror of death, till the Just God swept the warriors away by Moses' hand. The flood foamed, hunting them afar, bearing them off in its deadly embrace. The doomed men died. The sea fell on the land; the skies were shaken. The watery ramparts crumbled, the great waves broke, the towering walls of water melted away, when the Mighty Lord of heaven with holy hand smote the warriors and that haughty race. They could not check the onrush of the sea, nor the fury of the ocean-flood, but it destroyed the multitude in shrieking terror. The raging ocean rose on high; its waters passed over them. A madness of fear was upon them; death-wounds bled. The high walls, fashioned by the hand of God, fell in upon the marching army.

With ancient sword the foamy-bosomed ocean smote down the watery wall, the unprotecting ramparts, and at the blow of death the great host fell asleep, a sinful throng. Fast shut in they lost their lives, an army pale with terror of the flood, when the brown waste of waters, the raging waves, broke over them. The flower of Egypt perished when the host of Pharaoh, a mighty multitude, was drowned. The foe of God discovered as he sank that the Lord of the ocean-floods was mightier than he, and, terrible in wrath, with deadly power would end the battle. The Egyptians won a bitter recompense for that day's work. Never came any survivor of all that countless host unto his home again to tell of his journey or rehearse to the wives of heroes, throughout the cities, the grievous tidings, the death of their treasure-wardens; but a mighty sea-death came upon them all and swallowed their legions, and slew[1] their heralds, and humbled their boasting. For they had striven against God!

Then on the shore of the sea Moses, the noble-hearted, preached to the Israelites, in holy words, eternal wisdom and enduring counsels. They name it the day's work! And still men find in Scripture every law which God, in words of truth, gave Moses on that journey. If life's interpreter, the radiant soul within the breast, will unlock with the keys of the spirit this lasting good, that which is dark shall be made clear, and counsel shall

---

[1] Grein: *spilde*.

go forth. It hath the words of wisdom in its keeping, earnestly teaching the heart, that we may not lack the fellowship of God, or mercy of our Lord. He giveth us, as learned writers say, the better and more lasting joys of heaven.

This earthly joy is fleeting, cursed with sin, apportioned unto exiles, a little time of wretched waiting. Homeless we tarry at this inn with sorrow, mourning in spirit, mindful of the house of pain beneath the earth wherein are fire and the worm, the pit of every evil ever open. So now arch-sinners win old age or early death; then cometh the Day of Judgment, the greatest of all glories in the world, a day of wrath upon the deeds of men. The Lord Himself, in the assembly, shall judge the multitude. Then shall He lead the souls of the righteous, blessed spirits, to heaven above, wherein are light and life and joy of bliss. In blessedness that host shall praise the Lord of hosts, the King of glory, for ever and for ever.

So spake the mildest of men, in a loud voice, mindful of counsel, and made great in strength. In silence the host awaited his fixed will, perceiving the wonder, the hero's words of goodly wisdom. And he spake unto the throng and said:

"Mighty is this multitude and great our Leader, a strong Support who governeth our march. He hath given the tribes of Canaan into our hands, their cities and treasure, and wide-stretching realms. If ye will keep His holy precepts, the Lord of angels will fulfil the promise which He sware to our forefathers, in days of old—that ye shall vanquish every foe and hold in victory the banquet halls of heroes between the two seas. Great shall be your fortune!"

And at these words the host was glad. The trumpets sang their song of triumph, and banners tossed to strains of joyous music. The folk had reached the land. The pillar of glory had led the host, the holy legions, under God's sheltering hand. They rejoiced that their lives were saved from the clutch of the foe, though boldly had those warriors ventured under the roof of the waves. They beheld the walls upstanding. All the seas seemed bloody unto them through which they bore their armour. They rejoiced with a song of battle that they were safe. The army-legions lifted up their voice and praised the Lord for that great work. The mighty host in chorus, man and maiden, sang psalms and battle anthems, with reverent voices chanting all these wonders.

Then could be seen on the shore of the sea African maidens adorned with gold. They raised their hands in thanks for their deliverance; they were blithe beholding their safety; they took heed of the spoils;

their bonds were broken. On the sea-shore they dealt out the booty among the standards, ancient treasure and raiment and shields. They divided the gold and the woven cloth, the treasure of Joseph, the riches of men. But their foes, the greatest of armies, lay still in that place of death.

583-589

DANIEL

DANIEL

In Jerusalem, as I have heard, the Hebrews prospered, dispensing treasure and holding kingly sway, as well was meet, when by the might of God the host and all the battle legion were given into Moses' hand, and in a multitude they got them forth from Egypt. That was a valiant race so long as they might rule their realm and sway their cities! As long as they kept the covenant of their fathers, great was their prosperity! And God, the Warden of the heavenly kingdom, the Holy Lord, the Prince of glory, the Lord of every creature, watched over them, and gave them strength and courage, so that in war they conquered many nations who rose against them, until at last pride came upon them at their wine-feasts, drunken thoughts and devilish deeds, and they forsook the teachings of their law, and the might of God. So should no man sunder his soul's love from God.

Then I beheld that nation walking in ways of error, the tribe of Israel following after sin, and doing evil. That was a grief to God! The Warden of the heavenly kingdom oft sent His holy prophets, proclaiming knowledge to the people, and wisdom to the host. A little time they trusted in His counsels, till longing for the joys of earth defrauded them of lasting wisdom, and in the end they turned them from the laws of God, and chose the Devil's craft.

Then the Lord became displeased and angered with that people whom He had prospered. To them, a wandering folk, who once were dearest of mankind to God, dearest of all peoples and best loved of the Lord, He had showed a highway to their lofty city and their native land, where Salem stood, walled round about and girt with battlements. Thither the wise men, the Chaldean people, came up against the city within whose walls their wealth was stored. A host rose up to smite them, a great army, eager for deeds of blood. Nebuchadnezzar, the lord of men and prince of Babylon, stirred up strife against them in his city. In enmity he searched the thoughts of his heart how he most easily could smite the Israelites and take them captive. From south and north he mustered savage legions, faring westward with a band of heathen princes against that lofty town. The rulers of Israel prospered as long as the Lord would let them!

Then, as I have heard, these mortal foes, a host of unbelievers, sacked their city. From Solomon's temple, that glorious build-

27–59

ing, they took red gold and jewels and silver. They plundered the treasure under the walls of stone, all such as those earls possessed, till they had razed and wasted every stronghold which stood for a protection to that people. They carried off as spoil the treasure of princes, as much as was found there, cattle and men; and so returned, with great possessions, over the eastern roads, leading the tribe of Israel, a countless host, on a long journey unto Babylon, into the power of heathen judges. And Nebuchadnezzar showed no pity on the tribe of Israel, but made them subject unto him to be his slaves, all such as had escaped the sword. And he sent a great host of his thanes into the west to take possession of their kingdom and their wasted realm, after the Hebrews.

He bade his prefects seek among the wretched remnant of the tribe of Israel which of the young men they had brought there were wisest in the books of the law. He wished the youths to grow in knowledge, that they might teach him wisdom, but not at all because he could or would be mindful to thank God for all the gifts which He had given him to his comfort.

And they found three wise and noble youths, devout and young, and with the fear of God. One was Hananiah; the second, Azariah; the third was Mishael, chosen of the Lord. Stout of heart and thoughtful-minded the young men came before the king, where the heathen ruler sat rejoicing in his splendour in the city of the Chaldeans. And the Hebrew men with holy hearts spake words of wisdom and great learning unto the proud prince. Then the lord of Babylon, the haughty king, bade his thanes and princes on their lives see to it that the three youths knew no lack of food or raiment all their life long.

Now the famous lord of Babylon was great and glorious over all the earth, and terrible to the sons of men. He lived in insolence and heeded not the law. And there came to the great king in his slumber, when the prince had gone to his rest, a terrible dream that hovered about his heart, how wondrously the world was wrought, unlike for men, until the world's redemption. Truth was revealed as he slumbered, that there would come a bitter end to every rule and to the joys of earth.

Then the wolf-hearted lord of Babylon awoke from his wine-flushed slumber. His heart was not blithe; but a fear was upon him, and dread of the dream. Yet he could not recall what the vision had been. And he summoned his people, all such as were skilled in magic, and asked the men so gathered what his dream had been, while men lay sleeping. He was shaken with terror and knew no beginning nor word of the dream; but he bade them tell it to him. Troubled, the sorcerers answered (for wisdom was not given them to tell his dream unto the king):

"How may we divine so secret a thing in thy soul, O king! how thy dream hath run, or knowledge come to thee of Fate's decrees, except thou tell us first the beginning of thy dream?"

And the wolf-hearted king was vexed, and answered his wise men: "Ye were not so wise above all men as ye told me, saying ye knew my fate as it should fall, or I should find it in the future, nor do ye know the dream that bringeth wisdom before this people. Ye shall die the death except I know the import of the dream that lieth heavy on my heart."

But the company there gathered might not divine or search out knowledge, for it was denied them to tell the king his dream, or the mysteries of fate, until Daniel, the prophet, wise and righteous, and beloved of God, came to the palace to interpret the vision. He had pre-eminence among that wretched remnant who needs must serve the heathen king. God gave him grace from heaven through the communion of the Holy Spirit; and an angel of the Lord rehearsed to him all the dream, even as the king had dreamed it.

Then went Daniel at the dawn of day to

tell the dream unto his lord, recounting wisely the decrees of fate; and soon the haughty king knew all the dream, its end and its beginning, that he had dreamed. And Daniel had great honour and reward in Babylon among the scribes, after he showed the dream unto the king which the prince of Babylon had not been able to remember because of his sins. Yet could not Daniel bring him to believe in the might of God; but he began to build an idol in the plain which men called Dura, which was in the land of the mighty Babylonians. The city-warden, the ruler of the realm, reared an idol before men, a golden image displeasing unto God; he was not wise, but redeless, reckless, heeding not [1] the right. . . .

The warriors listened; and when the sound of the voice of the trumpet came to the city-dwellers, the heathen people fell upon their knees before the image, and bowed them down before the idol, and worshipped it, knowing no better wisdom. Wickedness they wrought and sin, with hearts perverted, even as their king. As their lord before them, the people turned to folly. Grim the reward that came on him thereafter! For he had sinned.

Now there were three men of Israel in the city of the king who would not heed their

[1] Grein: *rihtes ne gymde.*

lord's decree, nor offer up their prayers unto the idol, though trumpets sang aloud among the host. They were of the stock of Abraham's children, faithful men who served Almighty God, the Everlasting Lord in heaven above. The royal youths gave men to know they would not have or hold the golden image as a god, but only the Great King, Shepherd of souls, who granted them His grace. Oft they said boldly that they recked naught of the idol, nor could the leader of the heathen people constrain them unto prayer, nor compel them to go before the golden image which he had set up as a god. These thanes said unto their lord that this was their resolve: that they were subject to a higher power in this lofty city, " nor will we ever work idolatry,[1] nor worship the image which thou hast made to be thy god."

Then the prince of Babylon was angered with them, and in wrath gave them savage answer: grimly said that they should quickly worship, or suffer pain and torture, the cruel surge of flame, except they sought protection of that worst of demons, the golden image which he had made his god. Yet would the youths not hearken in their hearts unto his heathen counsels. They were resolved to keep the law of God and not forsake the Lord of hosts, lest that their virtue turn to

[1] Grein 2: *þis hæðengyld hegan.*

heathen folly. They had no longing to seek shelter with false gods, though bitter the death proclaimed!

Then the fierce king was moved to anger, and bade them kindle a furnace to torture the youths to death, because they withstood his will. The furnace was heated, as fiercely as might be, with cruel flames of fire. And the lord of Babylon, savage and grim, assembled the people, and bade his servants bind the prophets of God, and cast the young men in the flames. But He was ready who wrought them help! Though the prince so fiercely thrust them into the heart of the flame, yet a mighty messenger of God preserved their lives, and brought them help from heaven, as many learned. From heaven above the Gracious Lord of men sent unto them His Holy Spirit. An angel passed within the furnace, wherein they suffered torment, and covered the noble youths with sheltering arms under the roof of fire. And the heat of the quivering flame could not mar their beauty; but God preserved them.

Then the heart of the heathen prince was hardened; he bade them quickly be burned with fire. The flame rose high, the furnace was heated; through and through the iron glowed. Many a slave cast wood therein according to command. Brands they bore to the ruddy blaze. The ruthless king would

DANIEL

fain have built an iron wall about those righteous men, but the flame passed over them, beloved of God, and with joy slew more than was meet.

The flame passed by the holy men and fell upon their heathen foes. The youths were blithe of heart! Round about the furnace burned the slaves; the fire took hold upon those evil men to their hurt, and the prince of Babylon beheld it. Blithe were the Hebrew earls, praying to God with zeal and gladness in the furnace, offering their accustomed praise, because their lives were spared. With joyful hearts they worshipped God, in whose protection the fierce heat of the flame was turned away. The noble youths were sheltered from the flames' assault, and suffered naught of evil. The roaring furnace was no more grievous unto them than the shining of the sun. The fire harmed them not, but in their hour of danger the flames passed over them, and fell on those who did them evil. The heathen slaves departed from the holy youths. And the beauty of those cursed men was lessened, whoso had rejoiced in that work!

Now when the haughty king beheld how in that torture a miracle was come to pass, and believed his senses, it seemed to him a wondrous thing. The righteous men, all three . . . were walking unharmed in the fiery furnace, and one was seen there walking with them, an angel of Almighty God. No whit of harm had come upon them, but within the furnace it was most like as when in the summer season the sun shineth, and the dew-fall cometh at dawn, scattered by the wind. It was the God of glory who saved them from that peril.

Then in the hot flame the holy Azariah, eager-hearted, sang an inspired hymn. The sinless man praised God and spake this word:

"O Lord of all! Thy might is strong to save! Excellent is Thy name in all the earth, sublime and great in glory! Thy laws are always sure and just and mighty, even as Thou art mighty. . . . Wise and righteous is Thy will, O Lord of heaven! O God of spirits, grant us help[1] and favour! Save us, O Holy Lord! Wrapped in flame, we pray Thee for Thy mercy on our woe, our thraldom and humiliation.

"As we have wrought, so hath it come to pass. Our fathers also, city-dwellers, in pride have sinned, and broken Thy commandments, and scorned a holy life. We are scattered over all the spacious earth and driven asunder, cast out from grace. In many lands and under many peoples our life is infamous and vile, and we are subject to the worst of earthly kings, and captive to grim-hearted men; in heathen lands we suffer thraldom.

[1] Exeter MS., *purh hyldo* help.

"Thanks be to Thee, O Lord of hosts! that Thou hast laid this punishment upon us. Forsake us not, O Lord Eternal, for Thy mercy's sake which men attribute unto Thee, and for the covenant, O Lord of glory, Shaper of spirits, Saviour of men! which Thou didst give to Abraham, to Isaac, and to Jacob. Thou didst promise them in days of old that Thou wouldest bless their seed, and that a mighty nation should be born of them, a race to be exalted as the stars of heaven that trace their wandering courses even to the strand of ocean, and the sands of the sea-shore that form the foundations of the deep throughout the salt sea; even so should they be numberless for untold years. Fulfil Thine ancient promise now, though few are living! Show forth Thy glory and Thy word upon us! Make known Thy strength and power, that the Chaldean race and many nations living heathen lives may learn Thy glory under heaven, and know Thou only art Eternal God, Wielder of victory, Lord of hosts and all creation, the Righteous God."

So the holy men praised the loving-kindness of the Lord, rehearsing the strength of His might. Then was a gleaming angel sent from heaven above, with shining face and clothed in glory, who came to comfort and deliver them with loving favour. Holy and heavenly bright, he cast aside the blaze of the hot flame; with mighty strength he swept away and quenched the flame of fire so that their bodies were not harmed a whit. But in his wrath he hurled the fire upon their foes, because of their deeds of evil.

Then in the furnace, when the angel came, the air was cool and pleasant, most like the weather in the summer season, when rain falleth during the day and warm showers from the clouds. As is the best of weather, so was it in the furnace for their comfort through the holy might of God. The burning flame was quenched and scattered where Hananiah, Azariah, and Mishael, with brave hearts, were walking in the furnace, and the angel with them who preserved their lives, who was the fourth. Devout of heart, the three youths praised the Lord, and called upon the sons of Israel and all created things of earth to bless the Everlasting God, the Lord of nations. With understanding hearts they spake with one accord:

"O let the beauty of the world, and all Thy works, bless Thee, our Gracious Father, the heavens and all the angels, and the shining waters! Let all, who in Thy great creation dwell in heavenly glory, bless the Lord of might! Let all things made, the shining orbs that circle through the heavens, the sun and moon, praise Thee in their degree. Let the stars of heaven, and dew and the fierce storm, praise Thee. O let the souls of men bless the Lord of might! Let burning fire and radiant summer praise Thee. Let night and day and all lands, light and darkness, heat and cold, praise Thee in their degree. Let frost and snow and wintry weather and the flying clouds bless the Lord of might! Let the swift, shining lightnings bless Thee! Let all the earth, the hills and plains and lofty mountains, the salt sea-waves and ocean, and the welling springs, praise the Everlasting God, the Righteous Lord! Let the whales, and the birds of the air that fly in the heavens, praise Thee. Let all that move in the waters, wild beasts and all cattle, bless Thy name! Let all men praise Thee, yea! let Israel bless the Lord, who giveth all good things. Let holy men of heart, the spirits and souls of the righteous, praise the Everlasting God, the Lord of life, who giveth a reward to all. Let Hananiah and Azariah and Mishael praise the Lord! We worship Thee and bless Thee, Lord of men, Almighty Father, and Thee, True Son of God, Saviour of souls and Helper of mankind, and Thee, O Holy Ghost, the God of wisdom. We praise Thee, Holy Lord, and worship Thee with prayer. Blessed art Thou, and adorned with holy might for ever, above the world's roof reigning King of heaven, and Lord of life in every land."

Then Nebuchadnezzar, the lord of that

people, spake unto the princes who stood nigh unto him and said: "Ye beheld, my princes, how we cast three men to a fiery death in the blazing flames. And now, in truth, I see four men therein, except my sense deceive me."

Then spake a counsellor of the king, wise of heart and prudent of speech: "This is some marvel which we behold with our eyes. Bethink thee now, my lord, of what is fitting. Know who it is hath showed this grace upon the youths. They worship One Eternal God, and call on Him with zeal by every name. With eager words they praise His Majesty, and say that He alone is God Almighty, Wise King of glory, of earth and heaven. Call these men forth from out the furnace, prince of the Chaldeans! In no wise is it well that they should linger in that torture longer than thou hast need."

Then the king bade the young men come before him. Boldly the noble youths obeyed his word and came as they were bidden. The young men rose and went before the heathen king. Their fetters were burned away and the bonds of the king which were laid upon them, but their bodies were saved from harm. For their beauty was no wise injured, nor was any harm come upon their garments, nor their hair singed by the fire, but in God's protection they came forth gladly from that gruesome horror, wise of heart and favoured by the Holy Ghost.

Then the angel, a faithful servant to the Holy Lord, departed up to seek eternal bliss on the high roof of the heavenly kingdom. And by that marvel he had honoured those who had deserved it. The young men praised the Lord before the heathen host, exhorting them with words of truth, rehearsing many truthful tokens before the king, until he too believed this was a God of wonders who freed them from the darkness. And the mighty lord of Babylon, the haughty king, decreed among his people that he was guilty unto death whoso denied this was a glorious God of might who freed them from that death. He gave back unto God the remnants of His captive people and granted favour to his olden foes. And their prosperity in Babylon was great and their fame was known throughout the nation, after they endured that trial by fire, and obeyed their Lord. Mighty were their counsels after God, the Holy Warden of the heavenly kingdom, had shielded them from harm.

Then, as I have heard, when the lord of Babylon perceived the marvel that was come to pass within the flames, he was fain to know how the youths had passed through the blaze of fire, and overwon the terror of the heated furnace and the flames, so that the fury of the burning brands and raging furnace had wrought God's prophets naught of harm, but His defence had shielded them against that fearful peril. And the prince commanded a council, and summoned his people, and there, before the multitude so gathered, rehearsed the event as it had come to pass, and the miracle of God made known upon the youths:

"Consider now the holy might and wondrous works of God. We saw how He shielded the young men in the furnace from death and the leaping flames, because they served Him. He only is the Lord, Eternal and Almighty, who gives them glory and abundant weal who preach His gospel. And He reveals Himself by many a wonder to holy hearts who seek His favour. It is well known that Daniel showed me the interpretation of a secret dream, which formerly perplexed the minds of many men among my people, because Almighty God had given him an understanding spirit in his heart, and strength of wisdom."

So spake the leader of the host, the lord of Babylon, when he perceived the miracle and God's clear token. And yet he wrought no whit the better; pride ruled the prince. His heart was insolent and the thoughts of his heart were thoughts of pride, more than was meet, until the Lord Almighty humbled him, as He humbleth many who walk with arrogance.

Now a dream came unto Nebuchadnezzar in his sleep and troubled him. It seemed to him that there stood a tree upon the earth, wondrous fair, deeply rooted and gleaming with fruit. Nor was it like to other trees, but it towered unto the stars of heaven, so that it overshadowed the regions of the world and all the earth with its boughs and branches, even unto the shores of the sea. And as he gazed it seemed to him that the tree made shelter for the wild beasts, and that it held food for them all, and likewise that the birds of the air found sustenance in the fruit of the tree. And it seemed to him that an angel descended from the heavens, and spake with a loud voice, commanding the tree to be cut down, and the wild beasts and the birds to flee away, when its fall should come. And he bade that its fruit be cut off and its branches and boughs, but that the roots of the tree should abide fast in the earth as a token, until green shoots should spring again when God granted. And he bade bind the mighty tree with brazen fetters and fetters of iron, and thus bound cast it into torment, that his heart might know that a mightier than he had power of correction, against whom he might not prevail.

Then the earthly king awoke from his slumber, and his dream was ended. But fear of it was upon him, and terror of the vision which God had sent him. And the haughty king bade summon his people together, and the leaders of the people, and asked them all the import of his dream, in no wise thinking that they knew; but he made trial of them how they would answer. Then Daniel, the prophet of God, was called unto judgment, and the Holy Ghost was sent to him from heaven to strengthen his heart. In him the lord of men perceived an understanding spirit and depth of counsel, strength of wisdom, words of judgment. And once again he showed forth many a wonder, the mighty works of God, before the eyes of men.

Then the proud, heathen leader of the host began to tell his fearful dream, and all the horror of the vision that had vexed him, and bade him tell the import of this secret thing, bidding him speak in holy words and search his heart to tell with truth the meaning of the tree which he saw gleaming, and declare to him the decrees of fate. Then he fell silent. Yet Daniel clearly saw in the assembly that his prince, the lord of men, was guilty before God. The prophet paused; then God's herald, skilled in the law, made answer to the king:

"This, O prince of men, is no little wonder, which thou hast seen in thy dream, a tree as high as heaven, and the holy words, wrathful and full of terror, which the angel spake— that the tree should be stripped of its

branches and fall, where formerly it stood
fast, lying joyless with the beasts, abiding in
a desert place, its roots to remain fast in the
earth in stillness for a season where it stood,
as the Voice declared, and then after seven
years to receive increase again! So shall
thy fortune be brought low! As the tree
grew high unto heaven so art thou lord and
ruler over all the dwellers of earth, and there
is none on earth to withstand thee save God
alone. He shall cut thee off from thy kingdom and drive thee into exile without friends,
and thy heart shall be changed so that there
shall be no thought in thy heart of worldly
joys, nor any reason in thy mind save the
ways of the wild beasts, but thou shalt live a
long time in the forest ranging with the
deer. Thou shalt have no food save the
grass of the field, nor any fixed abiding-place, but the showers of rain shall drench
thee and harass thee even as the wild beasts,
until after seven winters thou shalt believe
there is One God for all mankind, a Lord and
Ruler dwelling in the heavens.

"Yet is it pleasing unto me that the roots
remained fixed in the earth, as the Voice
declared, and after seven seasons received
increase. So shall thy kingdom stand unharmed of men until thou come again. Take
now, my lord, firm counsel in thy heart; give
alms; defend the needy, and make atonement before God, ere yet the hour cometh

when He shall drive thee from thine earthly kingdom. Oft for many peoples God abateth pain [1] and woe, if they but earnestly repent them of their sins, ere His avenging wrath, with fatal doom, hath laid them low."

But Daniel was not able to speak these many words of truth, with craft of wisdom, to his lord, so that the mighty ruler of the world would heed; but pride ruled his heart. And bitter was his atonement!

And as the king of the Chaldeans ruled his realm, and beheld the city of Babylon in its prosperity towering up to heaven, the city which the prince had built with many a wonder for his people, and the fields of the Shinarites wide-stretching round about, then the king began to utter boastful words. He became perverse and arrogant of heart, beyond all men, because of the special gifts which God had given him, a mighty kingdom and the world to rule in the life of men:

"Thou art the mighty city, famed afar, which I have builded to my honour, a spacious kingdom. I will have rest in thee, a dwelling and a home."

Then the lord of men was smitten for his boasting, and driven into exile, arrogant of heart beyond all men. Even as in the days of strife, when God's swift wrath and anger smote him from the heavens, Nebuchadnezzar trod the bitterest path unto God's

---

[1] Grein 1: *wean and wyrcan.*

vengeance that ever living men have trod. Seven winters together the king of that fair city suffered torment, a desert-life with beasts.

Then the wretched man, companion of the beasts, looked up through the flying clouds; and he knew in his heart that there was a Lord and King of heaven, and one Eternal Spirit ruling over the sons of men. And he was recovered from the madness which long had been upon him, vexing the heart and soul of the king. His heart was turned again unto men and his mind unto thoughts of God, after he came to know Him. And the wretched man rose up and came again among men, a naked wanderer acknowledging his sin, a strange exile without clothing, and of humbler heart than the lord of men had been in his boasting. Behind its lord the world had stood, behind the prince his home and native land, unchanged for seven winters together, so that his kingdom had not lessened under heaven until its ruler came again.

Then was the lord of Babylon once more seated upon his throne; he had a better heart, a clearer faith in the Lord of life, knowing that God dealeth unto every man weal or woe as He desireth. The lord of nations was not slow to heed the counsels of his wise men, but far and wide rehearsed the might of God, where he had power of proclamation. He told his people of his wander-

619-649

ings, his far journeys with the beasts, until the spirit of the Lord God came upon him and thoughts of wisdom, when he looked up to heaven. Fate was fulfilled, the wonder come to pass, the dream come true, the punishment endured, the doom awarded, even as Daniel said aforetime that the king would suffer downfall for his pride, and earnestly proclaimed it before men, by the might of God.

Then for a long time Daniel gave judgment and counsel in Babylon unto the city-dwellers. And after Nebuchadnezzar, comrade and companion of the wild beasts, returned from his wandering exile, the prince of the Chaldeans, the wise and mighty leader of the folk, ruled his spacious kingdom, guarding his treasure and the lofty city, until death came upon him. And there was no man to withstand him upon earth till God through death took his high kingdom from him. Thereafter his descendants prospered greatly in that mighty stronghold, in the city of earls, enjoying wealth and twisted gold, a mighty treasure, when their lord lay dead.

And after him among that people arose a third generation, and Belshazzar ruled the city and the kingdom until his heart grew great with insolence and hateful pride. And the Chaldean rule was ended! For the Lord bestowed the kingdom upon the Medes

DANIEL 143

and Persians for a space of time, and let the might of Babylon diminish, which the heroes should have held. But He knew that they were sinful men who would have ruled the realm.

The lord of the Medes, as he sat in his stronghold, resolved on that which none had done before him, that he would lay waste Babylon, the city of earls, where the princes within the walls dispensed the treasure. Now the city of Babylon was the most famous of all the fortresses of men, the mightiest and most widely known of all that men inhabit, until Belshazzar in his boasting tempted God. They sat at wine within their walls, fearing not the hate of any foe, though a hostile folk with mighty hosts in armour were coming up against them, even against the city of Babylon to destroy it. And the Chaldean king and his kinsmen sat feasting on the last day.

Now when the leader of the host was drunk with wine he bade them bring the treasure of Israel, the holy vessels of the sacrifice, and the gold which the Chaldean warriors and their legions had captured in Jerusalem, when they destroyed the might of Judah with the sword, boasting exceedingly, with tumult seizing on the kindly folk and gleaming treasure, as they plundered the temple and the shrine of Solomon.

Then was the lord of cities blithe in his

heart, boasting fiercely and defying God, and said his gods were mightier to save, and greater, than the Eternal Lord of Israel. But, as he gazed, there came a dreadful token before men within the hall, that he had spoken a lie before his people. The hand of an angel of God appeared within the lofty hall, a sight of terror, and wrote before the eyes of men upon the wall in scarlet letters and words of mystery. Then the heart of the king was troubled within him and sore afraid because of the sign; within the hall he beheld the hand of an angel writing the doom of the Shinarites.

But the multitude, the host within the hall, debated what the hand had written for a sign to the city-dwellers. And many came to see the wonder. They searched the thoughts of their hearts to know what the hand of the angel had written. Nor could the nobles and magicians read the angel's message till Daniel, wise and righteous, loved of God, came to the hall. And his heart was filled with wisdom sent from God.

Then, as I have heard, the city-dwellers sought to tempt Daniel with gifts to read the writing and tell the import of the mystery. But the prophet of God, skilled in the law and wise of heart, made answer to them:

"Not for gain do I pronounce God's judgments to the people, nor of mine own strength, but freely will I tell thy fate, and the meaning of the words thou shalt not change. In thine insolence thou hast given into the hands of men the vessels of the sacrifice, and in them drunk to devils, which formerly the Israelites employed in holy rites before the ark of God, till pride seduced them and drunken thoughts. So shall it be with thee! Never would thy lord before thee lay hands of insolence upon God's golden vessels, nor boast thereof, although it was his legions that plundered Israel's treasure. But after the Lord of glory showed forth His wonders upon him, the lord of nations often spake before his people in words of truth, and said that He alone was Lord and Ruler of creation who gave him blameless glory in his earthly kingdom and great prosperity. But thou deniest that He is the Living God who ruleth over devils." . . .

747–765

CHRIST AND SATAN

CHRIST AND SATAN

The Lament of the Fallen Angels

It is revealed to those who dwell on earth that God had strength and power when He wrought the borders of the world. By His wondrous might He established the sun and moon, the rocks and earth and the ocean-stream, water and clouds. By His strength the Lord upholdeth all the deep expanse, and middle-earth. The Son of God beholdeth from the heavens the sea and its foundations; He numbereth every drop of the showers of rain. By His wondrous power He hath ordained the number of the days. Even so in six days, by His spirit's might, the Lord in heaven devised the valleys of the world and the high hills, and founded them. Who is there that clearly knoweth all that mighty work except Eternal God?

Joys He dealeth out and riches. He first created Adam, and a noble race, the angel princes, which later perished utterly. For it seemed to them in their hearts it well might be that they themselves were lords of heaven, princes of glory. Then a worse fate befell them, and they went to find a home in hell, the foul abyss, where they must needs endure grim woe and surging flame, no more possessing radiance of glory or high-built halls in heaven; but they must needs plunge downward to those depths of fiery flame, down to the bottomless abyss, insatiate and rapacious. God only knoweth how He hath condemned that guilty host.

The Old One crieth out of hell, with horrible voice uttereth words accursed: " Whither is fled the glory of the angels, which we should have in heaven? This is a home of darkness, terribly bound with fettering bonds of fire. The floor of hell is ablaze, and flaming with poison. The end is now not far when we must suffer torment, pain, and woe, no whit possessing bliss in heavenly glory, nor joy in her high halls. Lo! once we knew great bliss before the face of God, and songs of praise in heaven in happier hours, where now stand noble spirits round about Eternal God in His high hall, worshipping the Lord with words and works. And here in torment I must needs abide in bonds, nor ever hope for any better home, because of my insolent pride."

Then answered the foul fiends, black and sinful, chained in torment: " Thou with thy lies didst teach us not to serve the Saviour! To thee alone it seemed that thou hadst power of all things in heaven and earth, that thou wert Holy God, even the Creator. Now thou art bound, thou wretched fiend,

27-58

with bonds of flame. In thy splendour thou didst think the world was thine, and power of all things, and we, the angels, with thee. Loathsome is thy face! Sorely have we suffered for thy lies! Thou saidest that thy son was Lord of men. Now is thy woe the greater."

So with bitter words and moaning voices the sinful spirits spake unto their lord. Christ had cast them out, and banished them from joy. They had lost the radiant light of God in heaven through overweening pride. For all their joy they had the floors of hell and burning pain. Pale, their beauty marred, the fallen angels, miserable wretches, wandered through that loathsome pit, because of the presumptuous deeds which formerly they wrought.

Then once more spake the leader of the fiends; he was chastened anew, and racked with pangs of torment. Black with fire and poison, he began to speak; no pleasant joy was this as he poured forth his words in pain:

"I was once a holy angel, dear unto God in heaven, and knew great joy before the face of the Lord God, likewise this multitude. But I resolved in my heart to overthrow the Lord of glory, the Son of God, and have myself the power to rule the world, and all this wretched host which I have led unto a home in hell. Bethink ye of

58–89

the token and the curse, that I was banished, deep below the earth, in the bottomless abyss. I have led you all from out your native home unto a house of bondage.

"Here is no glory of the blessed, neither wine-halls of the proud, nor worldly joys nor angel throngs, nor may we have possession of high heaven. This loathsome dwelling burns with fire. I am God's foe. Dragons dwell ever at the gates of hell, inflamed and furious; they may not help us! This woeful house is filled with torment. In this deep darkness there is yet no place to shelter us, that we may hide therein. Here is the adder's hiss; here serpents dwell. Firmly the bonds of torment are fastened upon us. Fierce are the fiends, swarthy and black. Here never gleameth day in the gloom of hell-shadows, nor the radiant light of God.

"Once I had power and glory, before I earned God's judgment on my sin in this loathsome realm, upon the floor of hell. Now I have come, and brought a host of fiends, unto this home of darkness. But, flying forth from hell from time to time, I needs must visit every land, and others of you also, who had part in our presumptuous deeds. We need not hope the King of glory will ever grant us a home and dwelling, as He did of old, and everlasting power. For the Son of God hath power of all things, of glory and affliction. Wherefore, downcast and wretched, I must wander far, an exile journey, stripped of glory, shorn of virtue, bereft of joy in heaven among the angels, because I said of old that I was King of glory and Lord of all."

But a worse fate befell him! So the accursed spirit, doomed to woe, lamented his afflictions. (And through the foul abyss a flame of fire raged, with venom mingled):

"I am so large of limb there is no place in this wide hall to hide me, sore wounded with my sins. Both heat and cold by turns are mingled here. At times I hear the hell-slaves howling, mourning these realms of pain beneath the earth; at times men naked strive with serpents. All this windy hall is filled with horror! Never shall I know a happier home, nor any town or mansion; nor ever shall mine eyes behold the shining world again.

"Worse is it now for me that ever I knew the light of glory with the angels, or melody in heaven, where blessed souls are lapped in music by the Son of God. I may not injure any soul save those alone which He rejecteth. Those may I lead home into bondage, and bring them to their dwelling in the grim abyss. Changed are we all from what we were of old on high, in beauty and in honour. Oft, as disciples round our well-loved Lord, we brought the sons of glory to the Saviour's arms, and lifted up our songs of praise, and worshipped Him. But now I am stained with evil, and wounded with my sins. In hell-fire burning bonds of pain shall sear my back, nor may I ever hope for any future good."

Then once more the loathsome fiend from hell, accursed in his woe, bewailed his endless torment. His words flew up like sparks, most like to poison, as he hissed them forth:

"O! the majesty of God, the might of the Creator! O! Thou Lord of heavenly hosts! Farewell to earth, and the gleaming light of day! Farewell the bliss of God, the angel hosts, the heavens above! Alas! that I have lost eternal joy, that never again with my hands may I lay hold on heaven, nor thitherward lift up mine eyes, nor hear in mine ears the ringing voice of the trumpet, because I would have driven from His throne the Lord, the Son of God, and seized myself the power of majesty and joy and bliss.

"Then a worse fate befell me than I could well foresee! I am rejected from the heavenly host, cast out from light into this loathsome home. I may not well bethink me how I fell thus low, into this deep abyss, stained with my sins, and cast out from the world. Now I know that he will forfeit all eternal joy who thinketh not to serve the King of heaven and please the Lord. Needs must I undergo correction, vengeance and punishment and pain, stripped of every good, stained by my former deeds, because I thought to drive God from His throne, the Lord of hosts. Now, sorrowful and full of care, I needs must go an exile-journey, a wandering wide."

Then God's foe went to hell, wherein he was abased, and his thanes with him, covetous and greedy, when the Lord God hurled them down into that burning house whose name is hell. Wherefore let every man take thought in his heart that he may not be displeasing to the Son of God, remembering how the black fiends were undone by pride. And let us choose as our delight the Lord of hosts, the Prince of angels, and eternal joy in heaven above. He showed that He had strength and wondrous power, when from His lofty throne He drove that great host into bondage. Let us be mindful of the Holy Lord, eternal in glory, and choose a home on high with Christ, the Lord of all, the King of kings. With blithe thoughts in our hearts, and peace and wisdom, let us be mindful of righteousness and truth, when we think to kneel before His royal throne, and pray the Lord for mercy.

It behooveth him who dwelleth in these worldly joys to shine in beauty when he seeketh another life, and a land much fairer

156 THE CÆDMON POEMS

than this earth. That is a land of beauty and of joy, with fruits that brightly gleam among the cities. That is a boundless realm, the home of the blessed in heaven, acceptable to Christ. Let us turn thither where, in that dear home, the Saviour sitteth, Lord of victories, and round about His throne in radiant whiteness stand angel legions and all blessed souls, the holy heavenly hosts, and praise the Lord with words and works. Their beauty gleameth with the King of glory, world without end.

And further still, as I have heard, the fiends confessed. Their sin and punishment lay heavy on them. In their presumptuous pride they had forgot the King of glory. Straightway in other words they spake:

"Now is it seen that we have sinned in heaven, and now must ever wage a hapless war against the might of God. We might have had our dwelling in the light of glory, in thousands serving Holy God, and chanting hymns about His throne. And while we dwelt there, and abode in bliss, came strains of heavenly music on our ears, and the voice of the trumpet. Bright of word arose the Prince of angels, and all His saints bowed down before Him. The Eternal Lord Triumphant rose and stood above us, and each day blessed that gentle throng, and His beloved Son, Shaper of souls. And God Himself was merciful to all who came within that kingdom, and had believed in Him on earth.

"But it seemed to me that the Prince was stern and hard of heart; and I began to go forth alone among the angels, and said unto them all:

"'I can show you enduring counsel, if ye will trust my strength. Let us scorn this mighty Prince, the Lord of hosts, and possess us of the radiance of His glory to be our own. For this is empty boasting which we have borne so long.'

"And so it was we strove to drive the Lord from His dear home, the King from out His city. But widely is it known that we must dwell in exile, in the grim depths of hell. God holdeth His kingdom. He only is the King, Eternal Lord, Creator strong and mighty, whose anger smote us down. Henceforth this host must lie here in their sin, some flying in the air and speeding over earth. But round about each spirit fire burneth, though he be up on high. Yet may he never lay his hand upon those souls who from the earth in blessedness seek heaven. But I may seize God's foes, all heathen slaves, and drag them down into the pit.

"Some must needs wander through all lands, sowing dissension in the tribes of men throughout the earth. But I must suffer all things, in the pangs of flame,[1] sick and sorrow-

---

[1] Grein: *bitre* in *þæs brynes beala*.

ful, lamenting here my lost possessions, which once I owned, while still my home was in the heavens. Will the Eternal grant us ever again a home and dwelling in the heavenly kingdom, as He did of old?"

So wailed God's adversaries, as they burned in hell. God, the Lord, was moved to wrath against them for their blasphemy. Wherefore should every living man, whose heart is good, resolve to banish sinful thoughts and loathsome evil. Let us be ever mindful in our hearts of the Creator's might, and prepare a green path before us unto the angels. There is Almighty God, and the Son of God will fold us in His arms, if we on earth take thought of this beforehand, and trust His holy help. Then will He not forsake us, but will grant us life among the angels, and blessed joy. The radiant Lord will show us stable dwellings, and gleaming city-walls. Brightly shine the souls of the blessed, freed from sorrow, evermore possessing cities and a kingly throne.

O may we all proclaim it, ere it be too late, and rehearse it unto men upon the earth, unlock with skill the mysteries of God, and wisely understand them! A thousand angels shall come out to meet us, if thitherward we take our way, and have deserved this bliss on earth. He shall be blessed whoso scorneth evil and is pleasing unto God, overcoming sin as He hath said. The righteous, crowned with beauty, in their Father's kingdom, shall shine like to the sun in the City of Refuge, where their Lord, the Father of mankind, shall fold them in His arms, and lovingly uplift them to the light of heaven, where they may dwell for ever with the King of glory, possessing joy of joys with the Lord God, for ever and for ever without end.

Alas! how rashly did the cursed fiend resolve to disobey the King of heaven, the Comfort-bringing Father. With venom burned and blazed the floor of hell beneath the captive's feet. The fiends went howling through those windy halls, wailing their woe. The sin and evil of that multitude were fiercely purged by fire. Grievous their fate! And their prince, who came there first of all the host, was fettered fast in fire and flame; that was unending torment! For ever must his thanes inhabit there that loathsome realm, nor ever in heaven above hear holy joy, where they had long had pleasant service with the angels; all good things had they lost, and might not dwell save in the pit of hell, in that accursed hall where sounds of weeping are heard afar, gnashing of teeth and lamentation.

They have no hope but only frost and fire, torture and pain and swarming serpents, dragons and adders and a house of darkness. He who stood within twelve miles of hell might hear a gnashing of teeth, loud and full of woe. God's adversaries wandered throughout hell, burning with flame above and below (on every side was torture); oppressed with pain, bereft of joy, and shorn of glory, they bitterly lamented that ever they had planned to strip the Saviour of His heavenly kingdom, when they had their home on high. But He held rightfully the courts of heaven and His holy throne.

No one is so cunning or so wise, or hath such understanding, save God alone, that he may describe the radiant light of heaven; how, by the might of God, the sun there shineth round about that splendid host, where angels have eternal joy, and saints chant hymns before the face of God. And there are blessed souls, who come from earth bearing in their bosoms fragrant blossoms and pleasant herbs—these are the words of God. The Father of mankind shall fold them in His arms, and with His right hand bless them and lead them to the light, where they shall have eternal life, a heavenly home, a radiant city-dwelling, for ever and for ever. He shall have bliss whoso inclineth to obey his Saviour. Well shall it be with him who may obtain it!

THE HARROWING OF HELL

Within God's kingdom in the days of old the angel prince was called " Light-bearer," Lucifer. But he stirred up strife in heaven and turned to insolence and pride. Darkly Satan planned to build a lofty throne in heaven, with the Eternal God. He was their lord, the prince of evil. But he repented when he needs must sink to hell, and with his thanes must feel the Saviour's wrath; never thereafter might they look upon Eternal God for ever.

Then terror came upon them, and crashing thunder went before the Judge, who bowed and burst the doors of hell. And bliss came unto men when they beheld their Saviour's face. But the hearts of that doomed folk, that dread host named aforetime, were sore afraid.[1] They were smitten with terror throughout their windy hall, and wailed aloud:

" Bitter is this Storm that burst upon us, the Angel Prince, the Warrior with His legions. Before Him shineth a fairer light than ever our eyes beheld, save when we dwelt in heaven among the angels. Now will He end, by power of His glory, the torment we inflict. Lo! this Terror cometh, with thunders before the face of God, and

[1] Grein: *fagum folce ferhð geaclod.*

soon this wretched throng shall know affliction. It is the Son of God, the Lord of angels. He leadeth souls up out of hell, and we shall be abased hereafter by His avenging wrath."

By His might the Lord descended into hell, unto the sons of men. For He was fain to lead forth countless thousands to their native home. Then came the sound of angel legions, and thunder at the blush of dawn. The Lord Himself had overcome the Fiend; the deadly strife began at dawn when the terror fell upon them. He let the blessed souls, the race of Adam, mount upward unto heaven. Yet Eve might not see heaven until she spake:

"I, only, brought Thy wrath upon us, Eternal Lord, when we two ate the apple through the serpent's guile, Adam and I, as we should not have done. The fiend, who now doth burn for ever in his bonds, told us that so we should have blessing and a holy home, and heaven to rule. And we believed the words of the Accursed, and stretched our hands unto the holy tree and plucked its shining fruit. Bitter the price we paid, when we must needs sink downward to this flaming pit, and there abide for many thousand winters, dreadfully burning.

"Now I beseech Thee, Lord of heaven, by this host, the angel legions which Thou leadest hither, that I may be delivered out of hell, with all my kindred. Three nights ago a servant of the Saviour came to hell. Now is he fast in bondage, spent with pain, for the King of glory was incensed against him because of his presumption. Thou saidest unto us in truth that God Himself would come to all who dwell in hell. Then everyone arose, and leaned upon his arm, and rested on his hand; though racked with pangs of hell, yet in their torment they rejoiced because their Lord was coming unto hell to bring them aid."

And she lifted up her hands unto the King of heaven, beseeching mercy of the Lord for Mary's sake: "Lo! Of my daughter wast Thou born, O Lord, to help mankind on earth. Now is it seen that Thou art God indeed, the Everlasting Source of all creation."

Then the Eternal Lord let all that host[1] mount upward unto glory. But on the fiends He fastened bonds of torment, and thrust them down into the depths of darkness, bitterly abashed, where darkly Satan rules, a woeful wretch, and with him the foul fiends, forspent with pain. Never may they see the light of glory, but only hell's abyss, nor ever hope for their return, because the Lord God was incensed against them, and gave them bonds of torment for their portion, and gruesome horror, death-shadows dark

[1] Grein: *werud to* wuldre.

and dim, the burning pit of hell, and fear of death.

Then was there gladness when the host returned unto their native home, and with them the Eternal Lord of men, unto His glorious city. With their hands the race of Abraham, the holy prophets, bore Him up unto His home. Even as the prophets had foretold in days of old, the Lord had conquered death, and overcome the Fiend. All this befell at dawn before the blush of day, when thunder came, loud crashing from the heavens, and God bowed down and brake the doors of hell. The fiends' strength lessened when they saw the radiant light.

And the Son of God was sitting with His host, and spake with words of truth: "Wise spirits! By My might I wrought you—first Adam and this noble woman. And they begat, by God's will, forty children, so that a multitude were born thereafter on the earth, and many a winter men dwelt in their home, until it came to pass the fiend by deeds of evil brought God's mercy to an end. Now sin has spread through all the world!

"For in the new Paradise I placed a tree with spreading branches, whose boughs bore apples, and ye two ate the gleaming fruit according as the fiend, the thane of hell, gave bidding. Wherefore ye journeyed to the burning depths of hell, because ye disobeyed the word of God, and tasted of this horror. The foul fiend stood beside you, and gave you evil thoughts.

"But My heart repented that My handiwork should suffer prison-bondage! There was no power of men, nor might of angels, no work of the prophets, nor wisdom of mortal men, that could bring you help, but only God, the Saviour, who had ordained that punishment in vengeance. And from His home on high He came to earth, being born of a virgin, and suffered many tortures in the world, and much affliction. And many men, the rulers of the state, conspired against Me night and day, how they might slay Me.

"Then was the time fulfilled, and I had lived for three-and-thirty winters in the world before My passion. Long was I mindful of this multitude and of My home, that I might lead them up from bondage to their native land, where they may have God's judgments, and the glory of the heavenly hosts, dwelling in joy and knowing bliss of heaven, a thousand fold. Upon the cross, when sharp spears pierced Me, and the young man smote Me, hanging on the tree, yea! even then I interceded for you; and I came again unto eternal joys, and to the presence of the Holy Lord."

Thus spake the Lord of glory, Maker of

mankind, early in the morning when the Lord God rose from death. There was no stone so firmly fastened, though it were bound about with iron, that might withstand His wondrous might; but the Lord of angels went forth from His prison, and bade bright angels tell His eleven disciples, and say especially to Simon Peter that he might see God, Steadfast and Eternal, in Galilee, as he had done aforetime.

Then the disciples, as I have heard, were filled with the Spirit, and went together into Galilee unto the Holy Son of God, beholding where the Son of the Creator, the Eternal Lord, was risen. And the disciples ran and came where the Eternal Lord was standing, and fell upon the ground, and knelt before His feet, giving thanks to God because once more, as it was come to pass, they might behold the Prince of angels. And straightway Simon Peter spake:

"Is it Thou, O Lord God, crowned with glory? A little while ago we saw how heathen men laid grievous bonds upon Thee! And bitterly shall they repent, when they behold their end."

But some could not believe it in their hearts. And one, called Didymus, was dear before he laid his hand upon his Saviour's side wherefrom His blood had fallen to the ground, a bath of baptism. That was a glorious deed, the passion of the Lord our

God. He mounted up upon the tree, and with His great heart shed His blood upon the cross. Wherefore at all times men should thank their Lord by words and works, because He led us out of bondage to our home and native land, where we may have God's judgments and the glory of the heavenly host, and dwell in joy. To us the radiant light of glory is revealed, to such as have good thoughts.

Then was the Lord Eternal forty days on earth, followed of the people and revealed to men, before the Prince of city-dwellers brought the Holy Spirit to the great creation, the heavenly kingdom. The King of angels and the Lord of hosts ascended up on high. Then came celestial melodies in holiness from heaven. The hand of God appeared and He received the Prince; the Lord of heaven led Him to His holy home. And round about Him throngs of angels flew in thousands.

And it befell, while yet the Saviour Christ abode with men,[1] that on the night before the last He strengthened with His spirit His disciples, the twelve apostles. The Living God ordained unnumbered souls. Of these was Judas, who betrayed the Glorious Lord, our Saviour, to be a sacrifice. Little did that undertaking prosper when he sold the Son of God for silver treasure. The

---

[1] Grein: *mid niðum wunode.*

foul fiend gave him grim requital, deep in hell.

The Son now sitteth on the right hand of the Father; each day the Lord of hosts giveth help and healing to the sons of men throughout the earth. Full widely is it known to many men that He alone, by power of His glory, is Maker and Ruler of all created things. The Holy Lord of angels sitteth with the prophets in heaven above; the Son of glory hath His throne amid the heavens, and by His healing leadeth us up thither to the light, where we may sit with God on high among the angels, and have that radiance where His holy host now dwelleth, and live in joy. There is the blessedness of glory radiantly revealed! Let us take thought to serve the Saviour gladly and be pleasing unto Christ! There is more glorious life than we may ever gain on earth.

Now hath the Great Prince, the Almighty Lord, made intercession for us. On the day of doom God biddeth the archangels, with a mighty blast, to sound the trumpet over the city-dwellings, through all the borders of the world. Then shall men wake from the earth; the dead shall arise from the dust, through the might of God. Longest of days shall that be, greatest of tumults, heard afar, when the Saviour cometh, the Lord, with clouds surrounded, descending upon earth.

Then will He separate the fair and foul, the good and evil, into two companies. And the righteous shall mount to their rest at the right hand of God; they shall be blithe as they enter the city, the kingdom of God. With His right hand the Lord of creation shall bless them, and say before all:

"Ye are welcome! Enter now the heavenly kingdom, into the light of glory. There shall ye rest for ever without end."

But the guilty souls that have sinned shall stand and tremble when the Son of God shall judge them by His wondrous might; they shall hope they may ascend to that fair city with the angels, as the others did. But the Eternal Lord shall speak to them, and say before them all:

"Descend now quickly, ye accursed, into the house of pain. I know you not."

And straightway at these words hell's captives, cursed spirits, shall drag them down by thousands, leading them thither to the home of fiends, and thrust them deep down in the narrow pit. Never may they return, but there they needs must suffer torturing pain, imprisonment, and bonds, and the cold ground, endure the depths of hell and devils' discourse, black fiends with hate reviling them for sin, because they often have forgot the Lord, Eternal God, who should have been their hope. Wherefore let us resolve while in the world to serve the Saviour gladly by God's grace, be mindful of the spirit's joy, and how the blessed sons of God abide on high in radiant glory.

There is a golden gate adorned with gems, enwreathed with joy, for those who enter in God's kingdom, and win the light of glory. About the walls stand radiant angel spirits and blessed souls who pass from earth to heaven.[1] There are martyrs pleasing unto God, and patriarchs with holy voices praising God, the King within His city, saying:

"Thou art the Lord of men, the Heavenly Judge and Prince of angels! Thou hast led the sons of earth unto this blessed home!"

So the thanes about their Prince shall praise the Lord of glory. There shall be song and splendour round His throne. For He is King indeed, and Lord of all things in the eternal creation!

[1] Grein: *ferað to heofonrice.*

The Temptation

He is the Lord, the Prince of angels, who died for us; and, in the fullness of His mercy, the Maker of mankind once fasted forty days. And it came to pass that the Accursed Fiend, who was driven out of heaven and sank to hell, tempted the Lord of all creation, bringing in his arms great stones, and bidding Him make loaves to stay His hunger, " if Thou have so much power." But the Eternal Lord made answer unto him:

"Knowest thou not, accursed, it was written . . . save Me alone? But Thou, O Lord of victory, hast ordained the light for living souls, reward unending in the heavenly kingdom, and holy joys."

Then the malicious, evil spirit in derision lifted Him up in his hands, and set Him upon his shoulder, and ascended a high mountain, and placed the Lord God on a peak thereof:

"Gaze now full widely over the dwellers of earth. The world and the inhabitants thereof will I give into Thy hand. Take now from me the city and the shining home which I will give Thee in the heavenly kingdom, that Thou mayest truly be the King of men and angels, as Thou hast thought."

665–689

Then answered the Eternal Lord: "Depart, thou cursed Satan, into the house of pain; for thee is punishment prepared, and not God's kingdom. By most high might I bid thee bring no hope to such as dwell in hell, but tell them now of this, thy greatest woe, that thou hast met the Maker of creation, the Lord of men. Get thee behind Me! Know, accursed fiend, how measureless and wide and dreary is the pit of hell! Measure it with thy hands, take hold upon its bottom. Go, then, until thou knowest all the circle of it; measure it first from above even unto the abyss. Measure how broad the black mist stretches. Then shalt thou know more clearly that thou strivest against God, when thou hast measured with thy hands how high and deep is hell, the grim grave-house, within. Go quickly, that thou measure, ere two hours are past, the home allotted thee."

Then vengeance came upon the fiend. Satan, the cursed monster, fled away and sank to hell. And first he measured with his hands its torment and its woe. The black flame leaped against the evil spirit; and he beheld the captives as they lay in hell. And there rose a howling throughout hell, when their eyes fell on the fiend. God's foes had striven . . . the black evil spirit, so that he stood upon the floor of hell, and it seemed to him that from the pit to the doors of hell was an hundred thousand miles in reckoning, as the Almighty Lord had bidden him, for his sin, to measure all his torment. And he remembered as he stood in the depths of hell! The foul fiend with his eyes gazed through the loathsome den, until its overwhelming horror, the host of devils . . . then mounted up. . . . With words of malice the accursed fiends began to speak and say:

"Lo! thus may evil be upon thee always! Thou didst not wish for good!"

724-733

THE DRAWINGS OF THE JUNIUS MS.

WITH A PREFACE

BY

CHARLES R. MOREY, M.A.
PRECEPTOR IN ART AND ARCHÆOLOGY
IN PRINCETON UNIVERSITY

THE ILLUSTRATIONS OF *GENESIS*

THE illustration of the Junius manuscript was never completed, and in its present form is limited to forty-eight drawings scattered through the first ninety-six pages of the manuscript, which represent the scenes of Genesis. They were published with a brief commentary by H. Ellis in *Archæologia*, xxiv. 1832, pp. 329–340, and selections from them have been reproduced in the Palæographical Society's *Facsimiles of Manuscripts and Inscriptions*, ii. 14, 15. The reduced copies in the present volume are taken from the publication of Ellis.

The series has never had a thorough treatment, and the present chapter will in no complete sense supply this want, but is intended only to explain the peculiarities of the Anglo-Saxon style as manifested in these curious drawings, and perhaps to interest the reader in a phase of art which at first blush seems destined only to amuse.

For in truth the draughtsman's efforts leave much to be desired in the matter of naturalism. His billowy ground-line and impossible architectures are the very negation of reality, while the human figure assumes positions which make one ache to see, the drapery has no functional relation with the body, and the nudes are perhaps the worst in Christian art. "Adam and Eve," says Herbert, who devotes a paragraph to the Junius drawings in his *Illuminated Manuscripts*, "only become endurable when the Fall has driven them to adopt the wrinkled draperies which leave room for all the cunning convolutions of the Anglo-Saxon line."

And yet one can see in these rude essays a real sense of life trying hard to express itself through the medium of an inadequate technique; the artist shrinks from rendering no attitude or gesture which will help to tell his story. The whole of human action is his theme, and while his net result is usually ugly and lacks the petrified decorative beauty of Byzantine painting, there is in the work a realization, if not a grasp, of the actual, and the general trend of the technique is progressive and not decadent.

It is this aspect of Anglo-Saxon drawing—the initial phase of English art—which the present chapter will try to bring into greater relief, by means of a brief sketch of the evolution of mediæval illumination and the part played therein by the styles which sprang up in the British Isles.

The illustration and illumination of manuscripts is the mediæval art *par excellence*. Figure sculpture in stone practically died out in the fourth and fifth centuries of the Christian era, and was only revived in the twelfth century. Fresco-painting has large gaps in its history during the Dark Ages; tapestries

THE ILLUSTRATIONS OF *GENESIS*

come into view only toward the end of the mediæval period; and enamel, while it originated in the Middle Ages, found its highest development in the Renaissance. But the decoration of manuscripts was born and died with the Middle Ages; our earliest illustrated book, excluding the Egyptian examples, is the Vatican Vergil of the fourth century, and the invention of printing and the woodcut marked the end of real illumination. Hence it is that the successive phases and the inner tendencies of mediæval art can always best be studied in illumination; every century had its bookmen, and every book of importance was to some extent an artistic as well as a literary production. There is no break in the continuity of book-painting. From the charming little landscapes of the Vatican Vergil we make our way step by step to the beginnings of modern painting as they appear in the Franco-Flemish miniatures of the fifteenth century, such as adorn the pages of the *Très Riches Heures* of the Duc de Berri.

These vignettes in the Vatican Vergil, enclosed in simple banded borders and occupying half the page, of which the other half is given up to the text, are the final product of Greco-Roman painting. They still maintain the Hellenistic independence of formula; the little figures are conceived in three dimensions and movement that is fairly free; the modelling is bold, and the landscape has depth and a natural quality set off by the insertion of little classic buildings. In contrast to this Greco-Roman tradition of miniature painting there presently arose another

180 THE ILLUSTRATIONS OF *GENESIS*

in the Christian East, of which we have examples in the illustrated Coptic manuscripts of Egypt, and especially in the famous Syriac codex in the Laurentiana at Florence, known as the Rabula Gospel. Here we find new ideas—the Hellenistic half-page miniature is replaced by a full-page picture; instead of the simple banded borders we see a highly decorative arcaded frame which encloses the text and is supplied with ornament that a Roman artist never knew—birds and plants and geometric motifs native for ages in the art of Mesopotamia, and brought to life again by the revival of Persia under the dynasty of the Sassanids. Formality attacks the figure; free movement is lost and action returns to the single plane, parallel to the background, in conformity to the traditions of the pre-Roman East. Ornament, which in Greco-Roman hands was merely the repetition of an identical motif,—as, for example, in the egg-and-dart,—tends to become a running pattern which gradually draws into its scope the figures of the scenes which it encloses, with the result that they become more formal still. The perspective background of landscape or architecture which gave the illusion of real environment to the Hellenistic representation of episode, is reduced to a mere symbol of locality, a tree or a diminutive building, and then becomes a mere flat expanse of colour, merging finally into the goldfield characteristic of miniatures and mosaics of the style we call Byzantine.

Byzantine art, the art of the Eastern Empire

throughout the Middle Ages, was in fact the heir of this Orientalization of Hellenistic painting. To Greek tradition it owes the preservation of the human figure as its main vehicle of expression—in contrast, for example, with a purely Oriental style like the Mohammedan, in which the figure is eliminated; but Eastern influence reduced the figure to a strict frontality and a narrow type. It could only face the spectator or move in a direction parallel to the background, individual expression was denied the face, personal gesture is lost, and action confined to a few stereotyped attitudes and movements.

The result was the formation of a decorative style of high quality. The formality of the figure adapted it readily to every ornamental application, be it in mosaic on the walls and vaults of churches, or in miniature on the pages of manuscripts. This decorative merit, enhanced by the perfect Byzantine taste in colour and the skill of the Eastern artist in mosaic and the minor arts of enamel and ivory carving, gave Constantinople a remarkable prestige throughout the Middle Ages. Her artists, infinitely superior in technique to the "stammering craftsmen" of the West, dominated art in Italy till the thirteenth century, and largely influenced its evolution in the countries north of the Alps.

That Transalpine art did not fall completely under the sway of Constantinople, but began even at an early period to take on an individual aspect, was due no doubt in part to the precarious communication between the Western kingdoms and

THE ILLUSTRATIONS OF GENESIS

the Eastern empire, but also to the peculiar circumstances under which the mediæval styles commenced in Germany, France, and the British Isles.

In the latter, for example, we find the illumination of manuscripts practised at a very early period and in a highly original fashion. The Roman culture had taken no deep root in Britain, and Ireland was never Romanized. The Christian art, therefore, which followed the evangelization of Ireland, and was carried by Irish missionaries to Britain, developed without the Hellenistic traditions which conditioned the beginnings of mediæval art on the Continent. We find in Irish illumination an ornamental style based on old Celtic formulæ; natural ornament is excluded; the zigzag, interlace, and spiral are the chief motifs; and the human figure, while possibly owing something to the monastic art of Egypt, is utterly lacking in any trace of the Greco-Roman sense of form, becomes a series of calligraphic flourishes, and is woven into the linear design of the page in a manner that even a Byzantine artist could not have planned. The portraits of the Evangelists in Irish Gospels look like nothing so much as the kings and jacks of playing cards.

The Irish style, fully formed in the seventh century, spread into England and was there modified to some extent in the direction of greater naturalism in the drawing of the figure by contact with the Italian illustrated books which must have followed in the wake of Augustine's mission to Kent. A product of this Anglo-Celtic phase of illumination

THE ILLUSTRATIONS OF *GENESIS* 183

is to be seen in the miniatures of the famous Durham Book. But the activities of the Irish missionaries were not limited to the isles; we find them all over Europe, preaching the gospel to heathen tribes and founding monasteries from Italy to the Rhine. The style reached its height in the ninth century, and among the masterpieces of that period, the Book of Kells, produced in Ireland, is rivalled by the codices illuminated in the Irish foundation of St. Gall in Switzerland.

It will be apparent, therefore, that when the nations of mediæval Europe had reached that degree of national consciousness which demanded artistic expression—a phase which may be considered to roughly coincide with the foundation of the Holy Roman Empire at the end of the eighth century—there were four elements that could enter into the make-up of continental art: the Hellenistic or Greco-Roman tradition, the formal decorative method of Syria and Egypt, the combination of these two in the newly forming Byzantine style, and the Celtic art of Ireland and England. Of these the Byzantine was yet in a formative stage, and hampered in its development by the destructive iconoclastic controversies which wrung the Eastern empire from the middle of the eighth century far into the ninth, so that its influence on the Carolingian art of the West may be discounted, however much it counted in the later periods. On the other hand, the part played by the other three antecedent styles in the formation of the Carolingian can be unmistakably traced.

184 THE ILLUSTRATIONS OF *GENESIS*

In the history of art, the Carolingian "classic revival" has frequently been overestimated, both as regards the popular extent of the movement among the Germanic nations, and the nature of its appropriation of the antique. It is best understood as an artificial cult promoted by Charles the Great himself, and the eager students like Alcuin of York whom he called to his assistance in the spreading of the new propaganda. The ancient world, moreover, whose civilization Charles and his advisers sought to revive, was the last and decadent phase of the Roman Empire, not its apogee. Ravenna, not Rome, lived in the Frankish and Gothic mind as the imperial capital; the Carolingian ideal in Latinity was the language of Augustine and Jerome, the models in art were the decadent sculptures of the sarcophagi of the fourth and fifth centuries, and illustrated books like the Vatican Vergil and the fifth-century Genesis now preserved at Vienna. Hence it is that in the manuscripts produced for the members of the imperial circle at Aix-la-Chapelle the capital, or at Tours, where Alcuin had been given the task of founding a school of painting as well as one of letters, the classic forms reappear in the aspect of the Roman decadence; we find the miniatures of Tours faithfully imitating the banded borders, the architecture, and the landscapes of fourth-century models like the Vatican Vergil, but with a significant change in the drawing of the figure which will presently be noted more at length.

The artificial character of the Carolingian " re-

THE ILLUSTRATIONS OF GENESIS 185

naissance" is apparent in its lack of cohesion. It could not join the Oriental, Irish, and late classic strains into a new homogeneous and national style, but promptly produced a number of separate schools which are distinguishable from one another by the emphasis which each placed on this or that of the antecedent styles that served the Carolingian artists as models. Thus while at Aix and Tours the artists laboured to reproduce the effect of Hellenistic miniatures, we find in other places the birds and flowers and Oriental details of Syrian models like the Rabula Gospel, while the Franco-Saxon school which centred in the monastery of St. Denis at Paris, originally an Irish foundation, contented itself with a refined variety of Celtic ornament. Certain features are nevertheless common to all the Carolingian schools; the illuminated initial invented by the Celtic scribes becomes a fixture, the arcaded frames for the text devised by Syrian illuminators are always used in the "canon-pages" of the Gospels, and throughout the period we find a new and characteristic treatment of the figure—the one original contribution of the Carolingian style.

With all their respect for the antique, and for the prestige which Celtic Christianity enjoyed at this epoch, the vigorous races who had undertaken the regeneration of Europe could hardly be expected to find their ideal of humanity in the calligraphic designs which stood for men in Irish art, or in the animated puppets to which in the last phase of the antique the human figure had descended.

186 THE ILLUSTRATIONS OF *GENESIS*

According to barbarian notions, man in his ideal aspect was a being in violent action. Effective force was the Teutonic notion of human perfection then as it is to-day; the Carolingian discarded the "playing-card" types of Irish illumination, and was troubled by the inactive pose of his Greco-Roman models. Hence the peculiarities of the Carolingian treatment of the figure: the classic face is given a more racial turn with protruding eyes and high cheek-bones, the neck juts truculently out from the shoulders, the arms are always in motion. The legs are seldom left at rest, and here the artist, seeking adequate models in vain, devised the slanting "stance" which enabled him to render vigorous forward movement while at the same time avoiding the difficult problem of a spirited gait upon a level ground-line—a matter in which the slow-moving figures of the antique afforded him no guide. This accounts for the peculiar Carolingian base-line with its up-and-down drawing which makes the figures often look like giants striding across a range of mountains. The same desire for action accounts for the twisted pose of figures, which extends to those supposed to be at rest, like seated Evangelists or monarchs enthroned. The drapery, too, drawn in nervous fluttering outlines and flying folds, contributes its share to the general effect of vivacity. Whatever else of naturalism was lacking to Carolingian art, it succeeded in galvanizing the human figure into a semblance of restless energy.

This typical treatment of the figure, modified in

THE ILLUSTRATIONS OF *GENESIS* 187

other centres by the conventional influence of the late classic, the Irish, or the Oriental tradition, breaks forth unrestrained in the Carolingian school which had its centre at Reims. The masterpiece of the school is a manuscript of Psalms preserved in the University Library of Utrecht. It is a small folio of ninety-one leaves illustrated with 166 pen-drawings with occasional shading. The text is divided into three columns, and written in rustic capitals with only the initials in uncial, circumstances which indicate that the Psalter is a copy of an early codex. The drawings also seem to be based on a very early archetype, for those at the foot of the page refer to the Psalm on the succeeding page, the rendition of buildings is ultra-classical, and there are other occasional survivals of the antique. But the spirit of the illustrations is far from classic. They are literal to a startling degree; the phrase of the Psalmist, "Awake, why sleepest thou, O Lord," is rendered by the illustrator with the Deity ensconced in bed, surrounded by angels who vainly try to rouse Him. Everywhere the action is pitched in a high key of excitement: the figures pirouette and rush, the draperies flutter as if in a whirlwind, the heads protrude from the hunched-up shoulders with an effect of intense eagerness. The technique is remarkable in its illusionism. There is no continuous contour, but the figure is outlined by a series of right-to-left dashes — a method which materially aids the desired effect of whirling movement.

The Utrecht Psalter is the real ancestor of English

art. It was copied almost outright in England in three examples: the Harleian Psalter 603 of the British Museum, dating in the early eleventh century; the Eadwin Psalter of the twelfth century; and the Tripartite Psalter, now in the Bibliothèque Nationale at Paris (lat. 8846), of the thirteenth century. It had its influence also on the Continent, for as the artificial schools of the Carolingian revival passed away, the vigorous originality of the Reims style persisted, and, spreading finally into Burgundy and Southern France, it gave its nervous lyric character to the revival of monumental sculpture in the twelfth century, and inspired the pirouetting saints and prophets which adorn the façades of cathedrals in Burgundy and Languedoc.

In England the vogue of the new style, admirably fitted to the Anglo-Saxon temperament, was immediate and lasting. Celtic illumination had followed the Irish monks into England, but the art had practically died out during the miserable period of the ravages of the Danes during the ninth century, and when peace was restored under Alfred, the new continental style was ready to take its place. The influence of the Utrecht Psalter is seen at once in the popularity of outline drawing in the illustration of manuscripts produced during the tenth, eleventh, and twelfth centuries at Winchester and Canterbury, the two great centres of Anglo-Saxon book-making. A colour-style grew up beside the outline drawing; it is characterized by the same nervous energy and dramatic force, though this is dulled somewhat in comparison by the addition of colour. In the coloured illumination the typical Anglo-Saxon "rod-and-leaf" border appears—a combination of luxuriant acanthus leaves with a single or double gold band. Toward the middle of the eleventh century the two styles often seem to mingle in the same manuscript; a narrow band of colour is added to the contour of the figures, and occasionally we find a figure entirely painted in. To this may be added, as a further restraining influence on the exuberant vitality of the early Anglo-Saxon style, the petrifying effect of the developed Byzantine art on the drawing of Western Europe. This was never felt so strongly in England as on the Continent, but there is undoubted Byzantine influence on English iconography during the period, as we may see, for example, in the use of the pure Byzantine type of the Ascension in the Psalter of Athelstan and the Benedictional of Æthelwold of the tenth century, and it seems safe to assume that there is also a Byzantine influence in the technique. Whatever the cause, the Anglo-Saxon draughtsmen gradually lost the vivacity of the early technique which they derived from the illuminators of Reims; the outlines become more and more firm and continuous, stiffness and formality creep into movement and gesture, until the drawing finally merges into the hieratic formulæ of the first stage of Gothic.

It is to the intermediate phase of the evolution of Anglo-Saxon art that the illustrations of the *Genesis* belong. The style as we see it here has lost some of its early freshness, and gesture and pose are becoming fixed and prone to repetition. There is also here and there an approach to the colour-style, visible in occasional bits of shading, and one fully coloured figure (p. 204). The contours, too, are unbroken and sharp in the majority of the drawings, and lack the sketchy impressionism of the Utrecht Psalter; yet in this particular we find evidence of two hands at work in the illustrations, for the artist who drew the pictures which succeed the Flood (p. 235 to the end) adopts a different style from that of his predecessor, and one which frankly harks back to the style of the Psalter in the ragged edges of the draperies, the elongated figures, and the occasional substitution for line of the rows of little right-to-left strokes.

Both sets of drawings are obviously of the same date, however, and this date is not hard to determine approximately. Whether or not the ÆLFWINE whose portrait appears in a medallion below the "Deity's Wrath against the Rebel Angels" (p. 198) is the churchman of the same name who became in 1035 Abbot of Newminster, or Hyde Abbey, near Winchester, some such date and origin for the drawings is practically certain. While they lack the spirit and rapid technique of the Winchester works of the beginning of the century, and show the Anglo-Saxon style in a maturer form, the resemblance to works produced by the Winchester school in the early eleventh century, such as the Newminster *Liber Vitæ*, is still very close. The best figure to be found in the illustrations—the angel who closes the gates of Eden (p. 218) — has, as Herbert says, the "ingenuous fascination of Winchester art at its best." The architecture is often very close to that of the *Liber Vitæ*, with its Saxon windowed towers replacing the classic buildings of the Utrecht Psalter, and there is especial likeness in the drawing of the iron-work on the gates and doors. Elsewhere the artist reverts to the fantastic architectural perspectives of the so-called "Ada school" of Carolingian illumination (p. 217), and often his arches and framework are simply borrowed from the banded and foliate border of the Anglo-Saxon colour-style (*e.g.* p. 224, p. 226, and especially p. 239). It is from this source also that he gets the curious trees with their interlacing limbs terminating in acanthus leaves. In this respect and in the broadly vaulted structures like that by which he renders the "City of Enoch" (p. 221), the artist resembles the draughtsman who designed the Bayeux Tapestry which dates toward the end of the eleventh century, and a close parallel to the beasts and birds which decorate the border of the latter work can be found in the animals of Eden (p. 204). We shall not err, therefore, in placing the drawings in the second quarter of the eleventh century, and there is no reason why the Ælfwine of the medallion portrait should not be regarded as the patron of the work, and identified with the Abbot of Newminster of that name. That the text seems to be of the tenth century does not qualify this conclusion. The drawings do not reach beyond the ninety-sixth page; on almost every page thereafter to the end of the volume blank spaces have been left for illustrations, showing that the scribe expected them to be added subsequently. The manuscript was therefore written with space left for the illustrations; if these were added after a considerable time, it is only another instance of a fairly frequent occurrence in Anglo-Saxon manuscripts.

In treatment of episode the drawings show all the inventiveness of the Anglo-Saxon genius. It is true that no cycle of subjects in mediæval art shows greater variety of iconography than the Genesis story, but the Junius draughtsmen not only show the greatest divergence from other versions where the opportunity for comparison exists, but they have included so much in their voluminous illustration that many of the compositions are unique, and some of them, as in the History of Abraham, are hard to identify as to subject. In the story of the Flood, the traditional stepped pyramid, or *Ziggurat*-form of the Ark, is retained, which first appears in the Vienna *Genesis*. But the Junius artist was the first in the Middle Ages to give the Ark the additional aspect of a ship, a motif of course derived from the text of the poem, and reflecting the Anglo-Saxon familiarity with things of the sea which gives this section of the *Genesis* so vivid a character. On the other hand, Noah's " vintage " is translated in characteristic fashion into a scene of ploughing. The quaint touch whereby God Himself, or the Logos (He is represented here, as in the History of Adam and Eve, both with and without the beard), opens and closes the door of the Ark, was supplied the artist from the text.

The fact that the illustration is based on a " metrical paraphrase " rather than on the text of *Genesis* itself had much to do, of course, with the unusual character of the iconography. Here and there are reminiscences of earlier types, like the serpent-form assumed by Satan, in accordance with the text of *Genesis* and the tradition of Christian art, in two of the Temptation scenes, while in the other three the emissary of the Evil One assumes the form of an angel according to the poem. The dragon mouth of Hell is traditional in Anglo-Saxon iconography, though ultimately derived from Eastern sources, and occurs in the *Liber Vitæ*. In the History of Cain and Abel, the choice of scenes and their scattered arrangement on the page recall the parallel illustrations of the Ashburnham Pentateuch, a continental work of the seventh century, probably produced in Southern Gaul.

There are other reflections of earlier iconography with which I shall not weary the reader, nor risk impairing the force of the verdict already indicated —that the drawings show an inventive power, even considering the advantage they possess by being based on a highly imaginative text, which is equal to anything in Anglo-Saxon art. This is no small distinction, for the Anglo-Saxon is the most original of all the Romanesque styles, and contributed largely to the quaint realism of the Gothic miniatures produced by the Paris schools of the thirteenth and fourteenth centuries, whose art was strongly English in its initial stage. An interesting demonstration of this is found among the Junius drawings. A recent study by Mr. Dewald of Princeton (in *American Journal of Archæology*, 1915, pp. 277–319) has shown that the type of Christ's Ascension in mediæval art was derived from two distinct conceptions—the one Hellenistic and material, the other Eastern and mystic—and that by virtue of the persistent operation of Eastern influence on the artistic types of Western Europe, the original realistic rendering was finally changed in the twelfth century to an abstract scene wherein Christ hovers in the air surrounded by a glory and angels, with the Virgin and the disciples standing in a group below. But this type did not survive the twelfth century, for we find the Gothic realism transforming the type, so that Christ is represented as disappearing in the clouds of heaven, with His feet alone, or the lower part of His body, remaining still in view. Mr. Dewald was unable to find a direct prototype for this conception in earlier art, but it appears among the *Genesis* illustrations in the "Translation of Enoch" (p. 229), where the body of the patriarch is half concealed by the clouds of heaven into which he disappears. Such examples show the important part played by these primitive English craftsmen in breaking up the hieratic traditions of mediæval Christian art; it was their quaint but firm grasp of reality that first re-humanized art, and made possible the Gothic prelude to the rise of modern painting.

C. R. MOREY.

Frontispiece of the Manuscript of Cædmon's Paraphrase

The Deity expressing his displeasure with the Rebel Angels

The Rebel Archangel and his adherents   The Fall of the Rebellious Angels

The uprearing of the Firmament   The Spirit of God upon the Deep

The Saviour: The separation of Day from Night.

The Angels proceeding to Paradise   The Formation of Eve

God bestowing his blessing "Teem now and increase

God beholding the excellence of his Productions

Adam and Eve in Paradise

The Fall of the Angels   Satan in Hell

The Deity supported by Seraphim. Satan's Torment

The Serpent's counsel to Eve   Satan's Soliloquy   the departure of Satan's Messenger

The Spirit deceives Eve "Take thee this fruit in hand, bite it and taste."

Adam refuses Satan's temptation.

Adam deceived by Eve.   Their Sorrow

They are conscious of their nakedness and seek a covering

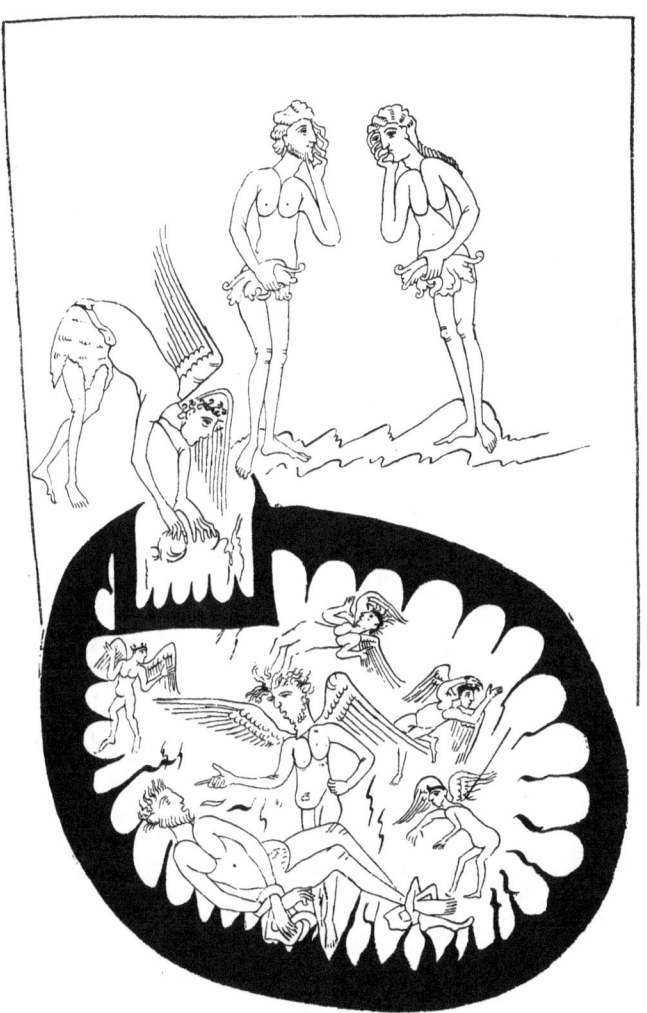

The fiends return to Satan.

Adam and Eve seek the "Weald": they 'sit apart to wait the Mandate of Heaven's King

The denouncement against the Serpent   God calls to Adam in the Garden

The separate Sentences pronounced on Eve and Adam

The Exile of Adam and Eve denounced, and their departure.

The Angel closing the Gate of Paradise.

The Birth of Abel

The story of Cain and Abel

Cain a wanderer he builds the City of Enoch

Members of the Posterity of Adam.

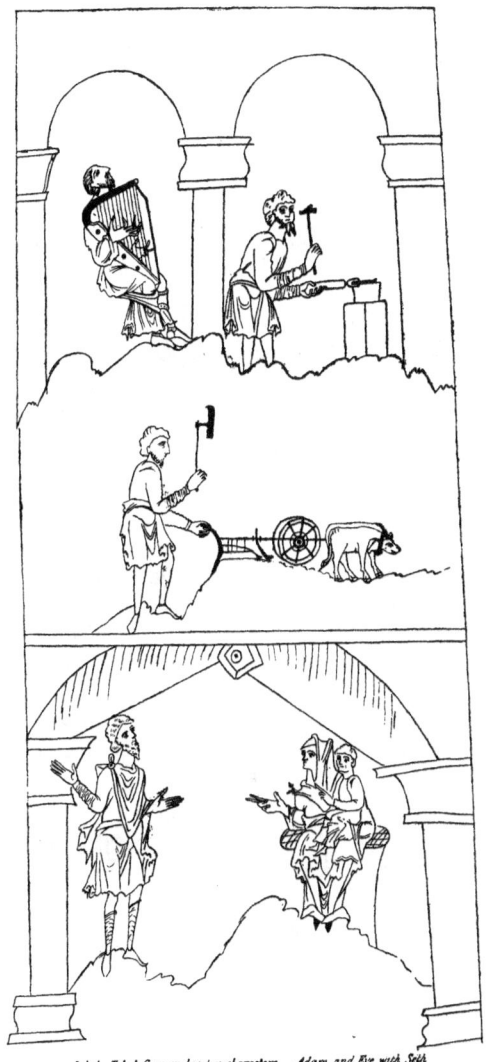

Jubal   Tubal-Cain in his two characters.   Adam and Eve with Seth

Seth in his prosperity

Enos the son of Seth, and his family.

Mahalaleel?

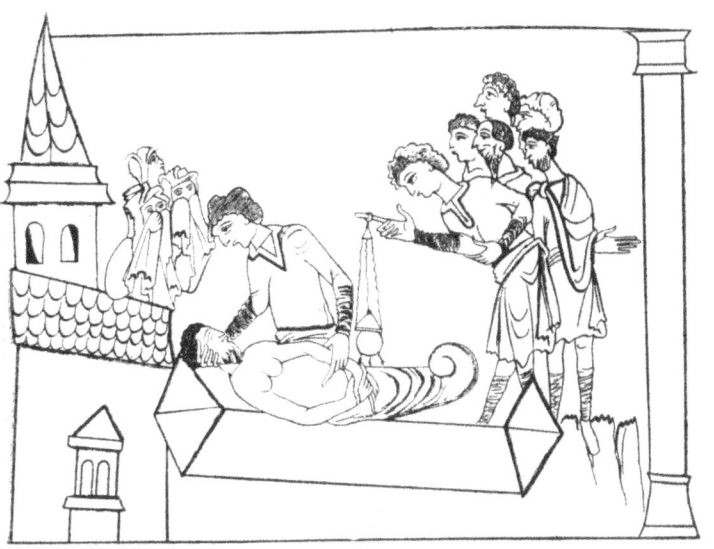

The Burial of Mahalaleel

An Angel conversing apparently with Enoch.

The Translation of Enoch.

Mathuselah and his Sons   The Birth of Noah

Scenes in the Lives of Lamech and Noah

God's command to build the Ark, and its commencement

The Ark completed.

The Ark afloat   God closing the Entrance.

Noah and his Family quitting the Ark

Noah's Sacrifice.

God's Covenant with Noah

Noah cultivating the Earth.

Noah's slumber and Ham's impiety.

The Building of Babel planned.

God's Visit to Babel   The Dispersion.

The History of Abraham.

Farther Events in Abraham's History

Abraham approaching Egypt

Unfinished Illumination

Ornamental Decoration on p 225 of the M.S

Capital Letters referring to the Pages of the Manuscript alphabetically arranged

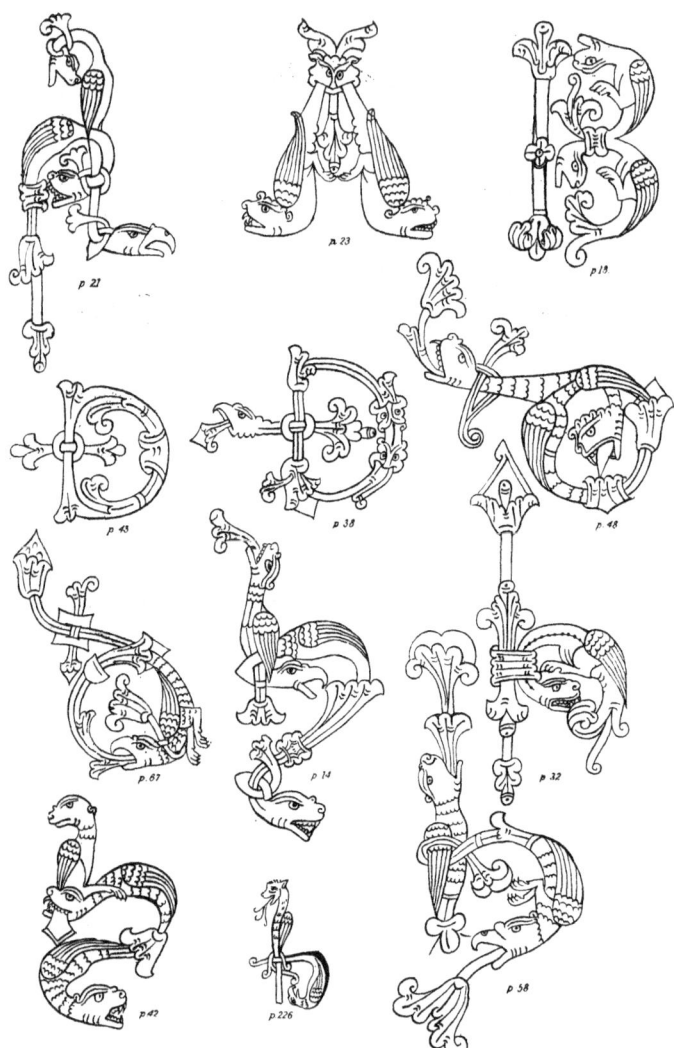

Capital Letters referring to the Pages of the Manuscript, alphabetically arranged.

BIBLIOGRAPHY

SELECTED BIBLIOGRAPHY

TEXTS

Caedmonis Monachi Paraphrasis Poetica Genesios ac praecipuarum Sacrae Paginae Historiarum. Amstelodami, 1655.

Illustrations of Anglo-Saxon Poetry, J CONYBEARE, ed. W. D. CONYBEARE. London, 1826 Selections, "Exodus," 447–463 and 490–495, accompanied by Latin and English blank verse translations.

Cædmon's Metrical Paraphrase of parts of the Holy Scripture in Anglo-Saxon, B. THORPE. London, 1832, with line for line translation.

Caedmons des Angelsachsen biblische Dichtungen, K. W. BOUTERWEK. Elberfeld, 1849. Followed by *Angelsächsisches Glossar*, 1851, and in 1854 by a third volume containing introduction, translation into German prose, and notes.

Bibliothek der angelsächsischen Poesie in kritisch bearbeiteten Texten, C. W. M. GREIN. Göttingen, 1857–64. Translation in alliterative verse, 1857–59.

Exodus and Daniel, edited from Grein, T. W. HUNT. Boston, 1883.

The Oldest English Texts, H. SWEET. London, 1885. Contains Cædmon's Hymn.

Angelsächsisches Lesebuch, F. KLUGE. Halle, 1888. Selections, including all of Exodus except vv. 362–446.

Bibliothek der angelsächsischen Poesie, R. P. WÜLKER. Leipzig, 1894. A revision of Grein based on new study of the MSS.

"Daniel und Azarias," W. SCHMIDT, *Bonner Beiträge*, xxiii. 1–84. 1907.

Exodus and Daniel, F. A. BLACKBURN. Boston, 1907.

Die ältere Genesis, mit einleitung, anmerkungen, Glossar, und der lateinischen quelle, F. HOLTHAUSEN. Heidelberg, 1914.

BIBLIOGRAPHY

CÆDMON

Bede's Ecclesiastical History, trans. A. M. SELLAR. London, 1907.
Anglo-Saxon Literature in England, J. PETHERAM. London, 1840.
Biographia Britannica Literaria, T. WRIGHT. London, 1842–46.
De Cedmone Poeta, K. W. BOUTERWEK. Elberfeld, 1845.
Handbuch der deutschen Literaturgeschichte, E. M. L. ETTMÜLLER. 1847.
De Carminibus Saxonicis Caedmoni adjudicatis, G. SANDRAS. Paris, 1859.
Ueber die Dichtungen des Angelsachsen Caedmon und deren Verfasser, F. GÖTZINGER. Göttingen, 1860.
"Ueber den Hymnus Caedmons," R. P. WÜLKER, *Paul und Braune's Beiträge*, iii. 348–357.
"Ueber den Hymnus Caedmons," J. ZUPITZA, *Zeitschrift für deutsches Alterthum*, xxii. 210–223.
Cædmon, the first English Poet, R. WATSON. London, 1875.
Der Dichter Caedmon und seine Werke, H. BALG. Bonn, 1882.
Early English Literature (trans. Kennedy), B. TEN BRINK. London, 1883.
Anglo-Saxon Literature, J. EARLE. London, 1884.
Grundriss zur Geschichte der angelsächsischen Literatur, R. P. WÜLKER, pp. 111–143. Leipzig, 1885.
Dictionary of National Biography. 1886.
Allgemeine Geschichte der Literatur des Mittelalters im Abendlande, A. EBERT. 1887.
"Cædmon and the Ruthwell Cross," A. S. Cook, *Modern Language Notes*, v. 153–155. 1890.
"The Name Cædmon," A. S. COOK, *Modern Language Publications*, vi. 9–28. 1891.
"Der Name Caedmons," R. P. WÜLKER, *Anglia Beiblatt*, ii. 225–228. 1891.
History of Early English Literature, STOPFORD BROOKE. London, 1905.
English Literature from the Beginning to the Norman Conquest, STOPFORD BROOKE. London, 1898.
Geschichte der englischen Literatur, B. TEN BRINK. Strassburg, 1899.

BIBLIOGRAPHY

Cædmon the first English Poet, R. GASKIN. New York, 1902.
" Geschichte der altenglischen Literatur," A. BRANDL (Strassburg, 1908), *Paul's Grundriss der Germanischen Philologie*, ii. Band.
English Literature; Mediæval, W. P. KER. London, 1912.
Von Kädmon bis Kynewulf, G. SARRAZIN. Berlin, 1913.

CRITICAL STUDIES

" Account of an Illuminated Manuscript of Cædmon's Paraphrase," H. ELLIS and F. PALGRAVE, *Archaeologia*, xxiv. 329–343.
"Collationen angelsächsischer Gedichte," E. SIEVERS, *Zeitschrift für deutsches Alterthum*, xv. 456–467. 1872.
" Zu Codex Junius XI.," E. SIEVERS, *Paul und Braune's Beiträge*, x. 195–199. 1885.
" Accent Collation of Cædmon's Genesis B," F. H. STODDARD, *Modern Language Notes*, ii. 165–174. 1887.
" The Cædmon Poems in MS. Junius XI.," F. H. STODDARD, *Anglia*, x. 157–167. 1888.
" On Codex Junius XI.," J. LAWRENCE, *Anglia*, xii. 598–605. 1889.
Älteste Christliche Epik der Angelsachsen, Deutschen und Nordländer, F. HAMMERICH. Gütersloh, 1874.
" Ueber den Stil der Altgermanischen Poesie," R. Heinzel, *Quellen und Forschungen*, x. 1–52. 1875.
Englische Metrik, J. SCHIPPER. Bonn, 1881.
Der poetische Sprachgebrauch in den sogenannten Caedmonschen Dichtungen, H. ZIEGLER. Münster, 1883.
" Der syntaktische Gebrauch des Dativs und Instrumentals in den Caedmon beigelegten Dichtungen," O. HOFER, *Anglia*, vii. 355–404. 1884.
" Zur Rythmik des altgermanischen Alliterationsverses," E. SIEVERS, *Paul und Braune's Beiträge*, x. 209–314, 451–545 (1885); xii. 454–482 (1887).
Die Altgermanische Poesie nach ihren formelhaften

BIBLIOGRAPHY

Elementen beschrieben, R. M. Meyer. Berlin, 1889.
Germanic Origins, F. B. GUMMERE. New York, 1892.
Die Metrik der sogenannten Caedmonschen Dichtungen, mit berücksichtigung der Verfasserfrage, F. F. GRAZ. Weimar, 1894.
"Beiträge zur Textkritik der sogenannten Caedmonschen Dichtungen," F. GRAZ, *Englische Studien,* xxi. 1-27. 1895.
"Anglosaxonica," P. J. COSIJN, *Paul und Braune's Beiträge,* xix. 441-461, 526 (1894); xx. 98-116 (1895).
A Contribution to the Comparative Study of the Mediæval Visions of Heaven and Hell, E. J. BECKER. Baltimore, 1899.
"The Influence of Christianity on the Vocabulary of Old English," H. S. MACGILLIVRAY, *Studien zur englischen Philologie,* viii. 1902.
On Anglo-Saxon Versification from the Standpoint of Modern English Versification, E. B. SETZLER. Baltimore, 1904.
The Dark Ages, W. P. KER. New York, 1904.
Textkritische Untersuchungen nach dem Gebrauch des bestimmten Artikels und des schwachen Adjectivs in der Altenglischen Poesie, A. J. Barnouw. Leiden, 1902.
"The Interpretation of Nature in English Poetry from Beowulf to Shakespeare," F. W. MOORMAN, *Quellen und Forschungen,* xcv. 1905.
"Zur Datierung des Beowulfepos," L. MORSBACH, *Nachrichten der Gesellschaft der Wissenschaften zu Göttingen, phil.-hist. Klasse,* 251-277. 1906.
"The Transformation of Scriptural Story, Motive and Conception in Anglo-Saxon Poetry," A. R. SKEMP, *Modern Philology,* iv. 423-470. 1906-7.
"Zur Chronologie und Verfasserfrage altenglischer Dichtungen," G. SARRAZIN, *Englische Studien,* xxxviii. 145-195. 1907.
"Die Sechstakter in der altenglischen Dichtungen," T. SCHMITZ, *Anglia,* xxxiii. 1-76, and 172-218. 1910.
"Chronologische Studien zur angelsächsischen Literatur," K. RICHTER, *Studien zur englischen Philologie,* xxxiii. 1910.
Zur Metrik des Codex Junius XI., R. WIENERS. Bonn, 1913.

"Notes on Old English Poems," F. KLAEBER, *Journal of English and Germanic Philology*, xii. 252–261. 1913.
"The Numbered Sections in Old English Poetical MSS.," HENRY BRADLEY, *Proceedings of the British Academy*, vii. 1915.

GENESIS.

Caedmon's Schöpfung und Abfall der Bösen Engel, J. P. E. GREVERUS. Oldenburg, 1852.
Der Heliand und die angelsächsische Genesis, E. SIEVERS. Halle, 1875.
"Cædmon und Milton," R. WÜLKER, *Anglia*, iv. 401–405. 1881.
"Zur angelsächsischen Genesis," A. EBERT, *Anglia*, v. 124–133. 1882.
"Studien zur angelsächsischen Genesis," E. HÖNNCHER, *Anglia*, vii. 469–496. 1884.
"Ueber die Quellen der angelsächsischen Genesis," E. HÖNNCHER, *Anglia*, viii. 41–84. 1885.
"Zur angelsächsischen Genesis, v. 431," J. M. MÜLLER, *Paul und Braune's Beiträge*, xi. 363–364. 1886.
Zur altenglischen Genesis, A. HEINZE. Berlin, 1889.
Studien über die Entstehung der nordischer Götter und Heldensagen, E. S. BUGGE. München, 1889.
"Parallelisms of the Anglo-Saxon Genesis," K. MERRILL and C. F. M'CLUMPHA, *Modern Language Notes*, v. 328–349. 1890.
Der syntaktische Gebrauch des Verbums in dem Caedmon beigelegten angelsächsischen Gedicht von der Genesis, F. H. SEYFARTH. Leipzig, 1891.
Teutonic Antiquities in the Anglo-Saxon Genesis, C. C. FERRELL. Halle, 1893.
Bruchstücke der altenglischen Bibeldichtung, K. F. W. ZANGEMEISTER und THEODORE W. BRAUNE. Heidelberg, 1894.
Der syntaktische Gebrauch der Conjunctionen in dem angelsächsischen Gedichte von der Genesis, G. K. STECHE. Leipzig, 1895.
"Zur Altsächsischen Bibeldichtung," T. SIEBS, *Zeitschrift für deutsche Philologie*, xxviii. 138–142. 1896.

The Epic of the Fall of Man, S. H. GURTEEN. New York, 1896.
" Untersuchungen zur altenglischen Genesisdichtung," H. JOVY, *Bonner Beiträge*, v. 1–33. 1900.
" Die Variation im Heliand und in der altsächsischen Genesis," P. H. F. PACHALY, *Schriften zur Germanischen Philologie*, ix. 1899.
" The Home of the Heliand," H. COLLITZ, *Modern Language Publications*, xvi. 123–140. 1901.
Der Heliand und die Altsächsische Genesis, O. BEHAGHEL. Giessen, 1902.
" Zur altsächsischen und altenglischen Genesis, v. 813," F. HOLTHAUSEN, *Anglia Beiblatt*, xiii. 266. 1902.
" Interpretations and Emendations (Genesis, 1351 ff.)," E. A. KOCK, *Anglia*, xxvii. 229. 1904.
" Ueber einige Beziehungen zwischen altsächsischer und altenglischer Dichtung," O. GRÜTERS, *Bonner Beiträge*, xvii. 1–50. 1905.
" Der Heliand eine Uebersetzung aus dem altenglischen," M. TRAUTMANN, *Bonner Beiträge*, xvii. 123–141. 1905.
" Legends of Cain, especially in Old and Middle English," O. F. EMERSON, *Modern Language Publications*, xxi. 831–929. 1906.
" A Note on the Sources of the Old Saxon *Genesis*," F. N. ROBINSON, *Modern Philology*, iv. 389–396. 1906–7.
" Zur Altsächsischen Genesis," W. BRAUNE, *Paul und Braune's Beiträge*, xxxii. 1–29. 1907.
The Epic of Paradise Lost, M. WOODHULL. New York, 1907.
" Die ältere Genesis und der Beowulf," F. KLAEBER, *Englische Studien*, xlii. 321–338. 1910.
" The Transmission and Date of Genesis B," G. H. GEROULD, *Modern Language Notes*, xxvi. 129–133. 1911.
" Milton und Caedmon," S. VON GAJSEK, *Wiener Beiträge*, xxxv. 1911.

EXODUS.

" Angelsächsische Studien : zur sogenannten Caedmonschen Exodus," J. STROBL, *Germania*, xx. 292–305. 1875.

"Zum Exodus," A. EBERT, *Anglia*, v. 409–410. 1882.
Composition und Alter der altenglischen, angelsächsischen Exodus, E. J. GROTH. Berlin, 1883.
Darstellung der syntax in der sogenannten Caedmonschen Exodus, K. E. A. KEMPF. Halle, 1888.
Germanische Altertümer in der angelsächsischen Exodus, M. RAU. Leipzig, 1890.
"Untersuchungen über die altenglische Exodus," G. H. MÜRKENS, *Bonner Beiträge*, ii. 62–117. 1898.
"Notes on the Cædmonian Exodus," J. W. BRIGHT, *Modern Language Notes*, xvii. 424–426. 1902.
"Translation of the Old English Exodus," W. S. JOHNSON, *Journal of English and Germanic Philology*, v. 44–57. 1903–5.
"Zu Altenglischen Dichtungen," F. KLAEBER, *Archiv für das Studium der neueren Sprachen*, cxiii. 146. 1904.
"Zur Quellenkunde und Textkitik der altenglischen Exodus," F. HOLTHAUSEN, *Archiv für das Studium der neueren Sprachen*, cxv. 162–163. 1905.
"The Old English 'Exodus,' ll. 63–134," A. S. NAPIER, *Modern Language Review*, vi. 165–168. 1911.
"On the Sources of the Old English Exodus," S. MOORE, *Modern Philology*, ix. 83–108. 1911–12.
"On the Anglo-Saxon Poem, Exodus," J. W. BRIGHT, *Modern Language Notes*, xxvii. 13–19, 1912.
"Relation of Cædmonian Exodus to the Liturgy," J. W. BRIGHT, *Modern Language Notes*, xxvii. 97–103. 1912.

DANIEL.

"Ueber die Entstehung des angelsächsischen Gedichtes Daniel," O. HOFER, *Anglia*, xii. 158–204. 1889.
Ueber die Interpolation im angelsächsischen Gedichte Daniel, G. STEINER. Leipzig, 1889.
Die Syntax des Verbums in dem angelsächsischen Gedicht Daniel, J. D. SPAETH. Leipzig, 1893.
"Zu Daniel, 266–267," A. NAPIER, *Archiv für das*

Studium der neueren Sprachen, xcviii. 397, and
H. BRADLEY, xcix. 127. 1897.
"The Anglo-Saxon Daniel, 320–325," E. FULTON,
Modern Language Notes, xvi. 122–123. 1901.
*Darstellung der Syntax im angelsächsischen gedicht
"Daniel,"* R. DETHLOFF. Rostock, 1907.

CHRIST AND SATAN.

Das angelsächsische Gedicht " Christ und Satan,"
K. F. GROSCHOPP. Halle, 1883. Also in *Anglia*,
vi. 248–276.
*Ueber die angelsächsische Gedichte von Christus und
Satan*, A. KÜHN. Jena, 1883.
"Jottings on Cædmonian Christ and Satan," J. W.
BRIGHT, *Modern Language Notes*, xviii. 129–131. 1903.
*Der syntaktische Gebrauch des Verbums in dem
angelsächsischen Gedichte " Christ und Satan,"*
J. O. L. WALTER. Rostock, 1907.
*Darstellung der syntaktischen Erscheinungen in dem
angelsächsischen Gedicht " Christ und Satan,"*
H. E. W. MEYER. Rostock, 1907.
"Interpretations and Emendations (Christ and
Satan, 273–276)," E. A. KOCK, *Anglia*, xxvii.
229. 1904.
"The Old English Gospel of Nicodemus," W. H.
HULME, *Modern Language Publications*, xiii.
457–542 (1898), and *Modern Philology*, i.
579–614 (1903–4).
"Quellen und Verwandtschaften der älteren ger-
manischen Darstellungen des Jüngsten Ger-
ichtes," G. GRAU, *Studien zur englischen
Philologie*, xxxi. 1908.
"Christ und Satan," T. FRINGS, *Zeitschrift für
deutsche Philologie*, xlv. 217–236. 1913–14.